ETHNICITY
AND
CITIZENSHIP
The Canadian Case

edited by
JEAN LAPONCE and WILLIAM SAFRAN

FRANK CASS • LONDON

First published in 1996 in Great Britain by
FRANK CASS & CO. LTD
Newbury House, 900 Eastern Avenue, London IG2 7HH, England

and in the United States of America by
FRANK CASS
c/o ISBS
5804 N.E. Hassalo Street
Portland, Oregon 97213-3644

Transferred to Digital Printing 2004

Library of Congress Cataloging-in-Publication Data

Ethnicity and citizenship: the Canadian case/edited by Jean A.
Laponce and William Safran.
    p.   cm.
"First appeared in a special issue of Nationalism & ethnic
politics, volume 1, number 3, autumn 1995"--t.p. verso.
Includes bibliographical references and index.
    ISBN 0-7146-4693-8 (cloth). -- ISBN 0-7146-4231-2 (pbk.)
    1. Ethnicity--Canada. 2 Citizenship--Canada.
3. Multiculturalism--Canada. 4. Canada--Ethnic relations.
5. Canada--Politics and government. I. Laponce, J.A. II. Safran,
William.
F1035.A1E8725 1995   95-33459
305.8'00971--dc20   CIP

Library of Congress Cataloging-in-Publication Data

This group of articles first appeared in a special issue of *Nationalism & Ethnic
Politics*, Volume 1, Number 3, Autumn 1995, published by Frank Cass & Co. Ltd.
(Ethnicity and Citizenship: the Canadian Case)

Typeset by Frank Cass & Co. Ltd., London

Contents

Ethnicity and Citizenship as Generators of Each Other: the Canadian Case

J.A. LAPONCE

In his study of power involving two genies assumed to hide in all political systems, Guglielmo Ferrero remarks that humanity has invented only two ways of structuring mentally the origins of authority: it sees it coming either from above or from below.[1] The same can be said, with the qualifications appropriate to academic discourse, of the contemporary debate over the nature of ethnicity and nationalism.[2] Under the terms of 'ethnic' and 'civic', 'primordial' and 'constructed', and other such labels, the students of ethnic and national identity typically give prominence, in their explanations, to one of the two genies that cohabit sometimes harmoniously, but often quarrel, and often succeed in involving in their quarrels the observer who meant to remain impartial.

To illustrate some aspects of the collaboration and conflict between national and ethnic genies, between those from above and those from below, this volume takes Canada as a test case and focuses on the relationship between ethnicity and citizenship.

The articles that follow were first read, in the spring of 1994, at a conference organized by the Royal Society of Canada and the Institute of Interethnic Relations of the University of Ottawa. The authors were given the general theme summarized in the title of this Introduction but no specific marching orders; they were left free to relate the theme to their specific disciplines and research interests: History in the case of Craig Brown, Public Law and the Constitution in the case of Peter Russell, Women's Studies and Feminist theory in the case of Caroline Andrew, the sociology of ethnic relations in the case of Leslie Laczko, the measuring of psychological ethnic distance in the case of Rudolph Kalin, and finally, Québec political culture and ideologies in the case of Louis Balthazar.

We shall use this Introduction to offer a brief description of Canada's ethnic situation and use it also to test the applicability of a general typology that relates different kinds of ethnos to different kinds of citizenship. To do so we shall draw on two different sets of data: objective data offered by the census, and subjective data obtained from survey research.

Types of citizenship and types of ethnic community

Let us distinguish two types of citizenship that need not be exclusive of each other: the legal citizenship studied by Peter Russell and Craig Brown, and the societal citizenship to which Louis Balthazar draws our attention in the case of Québec. Let us also distinguish at least three major types of ethnic groups and collective identities: the pan-state, the embedded, and the separate, which we shall treat, at the outset, as exclusive of one another in order to simplify the model (see Table 1).

TABLE 1
TYPES OF ETHNIC AND CITIZENSHIP COMMUNITIES

Types of ethnic groups

	pan-state	embedded	separate
legal			
societal			

Types of Citizenship

The legal citizenship is easier to describe than the societal. The right to a passport and the right to vote (after a certain age) are now almost universally associated with citizenship in democratic states. In the Canadian case, the right to a passport is a good and simple marker of citizenship. That right is of relatively easy access to outsiders. With a total population of 26 million, Canada has, for the past decade, taken an average of 150,000 migrants per year (the 1994 target of 250,000 was reduced to 182,000 for 1995).[3] The sources of that immigration have changed markedly since the 1960s. Then they were overwhelmingly European, now they are primarily Asian. Thus, Canada's population becomes increasingly diversified.[4]

Immigrants have the option of becoming citizens after only three years of residence. Does a legal citizenship so easily granted generate a societal citizenship – does it generate a sense of ethnic solidarity? The evidence presented by Rudolph Kalin and Leslie Laczko shows that it does; the spill-over from the legal to the societal is particularly high among newcomers and these newcomers are relatively well accepted. The resistance to translating the legal into the social does not come from the recent immigrants but from the two ethnic communities that are older and have retained a sense of being older than the Canadian state: the Québécois and the Aboriginals.

Paradoxically, the ease with which the newcomers, as distinct from the first and second nations, become and feel Canadian is probably facilitated by Canada allowing dual, indeed multiple, citizenships. Allegiance to a new state is probably made easier if the new allegiance is not exclusive of an older one that is let to fade naturally into the background. A test of the importance of this tolerance may come on the occasion of the 1995 Québec referendum, the Parti Québécois having announced that, should Québec vote in favour of separation from Canada, its citizens would be allowed to keep their Canadian citizenship. Would the federal government, as suggested by some commentators, wish to deny that possibility? If it did, would it deprive itself, like Germany, of what I assume is an effective means of integration and assimilation?

The three types of ethnic groups distinguished by Table 1 depart from the more commonly used typologies. An explanation is thus in order. Following Walker Connor's recommendation,[5] I use the term 'pan-state' rather than 'national' to describe the ethnic group – here the politically dominant group – whose collective identity coincides with that given by the state's citizenship. There are still remnants, notably among French Canadians outside Québec, of the ideal of a two-nation state – French and English – that would co-govern from coast to coast, but that ideal having been abandoned by Québec, and the Aboriginals still being fragmented by tribal and language loyalties, there is now, by and large, only one group that fits our pan-state category, that which will be identified by the survey data, very simply, as 'Canadian'.

The embedded category refers to individuals and communities frequently described by the term 'hyphenated Canadians' who – Russian doll style – have a second-order ethnic identity set within their overarching Canadian self, Canadian-Ukrainian or German-Canadian, for example. The hierarchy of embededness could of course be the reverse of that we just described. There must be cases where the Canadian identity is of the second rather than of the first order. The limited evidence available indicates that this second type of embeddedness is far less frequent than the first.

Furthermore, the case of a Canadian identity subordinated to another ethnos has hierarchical features that make it resemble the category we call 'separate'. For that reason we shall treat the 'Canadian second order' case as a variety of the 'separate' category in order to simplify the models presented by Tables 2 and 3.[6]

The category 'separate ethnic identity' refers to individuals whose dominant ethnic identity is other than Canadian.[7] These individuals may and will usually have Canadian legal citizenship but will not share, or share only to a limited extent, their societal citizenship with other Canadians. Many Québécois and Indians belong to this category, especially Indians who live on reserves regulated by many different definitions of membership (societal citizenship) specific to each tribal community.[8]

The Canadian ethnic equilibrium: comparing census and survey data.

Before putting names and numbers in the cells of Table 1, let us consider – if only to show how misleading official statistics can be – the data that is commonly used to describe Canada as an extreme case of multi-ethnic and multicultural society.

The Canadian census tells us that the two founding 'races' that Lord Durham recommended merging and that André Siegfried saw 'in conflict' within a single state[9] – the French and the English – have lost considerable ground to the 'new' Canadians. They dropped from over 90 per cent in 1871 to less than 51 per cent in 1991 (see Table 2). The same statistics also tell us that, in 1991, the number of individuals who identified their origins as either British, English, Scottish, Welsh, or Irish was not much higher than the number of those with a French origin (28 per cent compared to 23 per cent).

This first reading of Table 2 needs to be immediately qualified and corrected. The left side of the Table, that which covers the first hundred years since the creation of the Canadian state in 1867, can be compared to the right side of the same Table (which covers the years 1981 and 1991) provided we take into consideration a change in the census question that occurred in 1981. Before that date, in addition to obliging the respondent to trace their origins outside Canada and the United States, the census questionnaire compelled the use of single answers. People could not be Ukrainian-English, they had to be either Ukrainian or English. Starting in 1981 the census made it possible to indicate multiple origins by adding an open-ended question after the listing of the more common single entries (such as English, French, Italian). The open-ended question said ' if other, specify.....' In 1981, only 1.3 per cent of respondents used that new possibility; in 1991, 29 per cent did so, many of them in order to list multiple origins. It is revealing that the change in the wording of the question caused a sharp drop in the category 'British' but only a minor one in the category 'French'. This difference comes from markedly different rates of ethnic endogamy. The social boundary defined by ethnic origin is markedly higher for the 'French' than for the 'British'. It is also revealing that the individuals of mixed 'British and other' ancestry, when forced to make a choice, prior to 1981, had so frequently chosen 'British'. Whatever the cause of that preference (surname, language, political institutions, culture?), the outcome is clear: in Canada, ethnic identification is often subject to a Gresham law in reverse; the dominant, the 'better' identification tends to drive out the 'weaker' ones.[8]

TABLE 2
THE CANADIAN POPULATION BY ETHNIC ORIGIN AS MEASURED BY THE CENSUS*

	1871	1971	1981	1991
British Isles**	61	45	40	28
French	31	29	27	23
Other European	7	23	19	15
Asian		1	3	5
other (single)	1	2	(single) 3	7***
			(multiple) 8	22****

* For the period 1871–1971 and intermediate years see Warren Kalbach "A Demographic Overview of Racial and Ethnic Groups in Canada" in Peter S. Li (ed.) *Race and Ethnic Relations in Canada* (Toronto: Toronto University Press, 1990) pp.18–50. For 1991 see *the Ethnic Population of Canada* (Ottawa: Supply and Services, n 315, 1993).

** The category British includes single and multiple origins, such as English-Scottish. The multiple origins within the category amount to 7%.

*** The single origin in 'Canadian' was volunteered 3% of the time, and the term 'Canadian' appeared 1% of the time as part of multiple answers, although such inclusion was discouraged by the question which asked for the origins of one's ancestors.

**** Not including the 7% of mixed origins from within the British Isles.

But even after the reform of 1981, the census continues to be misleading whenever we use it to translate ethnic origin into ethnic identification. The recent censuses tell us that the Canadian population has very diverse origins, that it has many potential ethnic fault lines. It does not tell us where the ethnic cleavages actually run. To get closer to the desired picture, we must turn to survey data of personal attitudes.

TABLE 3

CANADA'S MAJOR ETHNIC GROUPS BY TYPES OF CITIZENSHIP AND SELF IDENTIFICATION*

Type of ethnic group

		pan-state overarching	embedded	separate
Types of Citizenship	legal			Québécois 14% Maritimes 12% Other prov. 1% Other countries 4%
	legal + societal	Canadian 65%	Hypenated Canadians 13%	

* The classification and the percentages are derived from the survey data described in the text and footnote 11. All hyphenated Canadians have been assumed to fall in the 'societal' category of Canadian citizenship. That is probably a slight exaggeration. All the respondents who had indicated either their province or a foreign country as the best describer of their identity have been assigned to the legal, non-societal, type of citizenship. That is probably a more serious exaggeration, especially for the identifiers with provinces other than Quebec. See the text for suggested corrections.

The Aboriginals did not appear as a separate category in the data used for building the Table. Their number is variously estimated from 2% to 4% of the total population. Taking into account their high exogamy rates (over 50%) their contribution to the 'separate-legal' category is probably around 1% to 2%.

Let us do so by using the survey from which Laczko and Kalin derive their observations. That survey, in addition to identifying the ethnic origin of the subjects interviewed, gave the respondents the possibility of describing the self either by origin, by province, by hyphenated combination, or simply as 'Canadian' (see the exact wording of the question on page 30). The inclusion of 'Canadian' as a possible answer enables us to identify more accurately the workings of the anti-Gresham law of ethnic identification. The results are unequivocal. The identification 'British' (including its components: English, Welsh, Scottish, Irish), and the identification 'French' practically disappear (1 per cent of the total population each). The composites 'British-Canadian' and 'French-Canadian' do not score much higher (3 per cent and 4 per cent respectively). The major ethnic cleavage identified by the question is between 'Canadians' and 'Québécois'. That may not seem to be a startling finding, yet it is one that does not appear to have been taken to its unavoidable conclusion by the politicians and analysts who, faced with Québec's constant demands for more power, ask and wonder, 'Who speaks for English Canada?' There is no English Canada. The dominant group does not see itself as being English or British, and is hardly conscious of being Anglophone;[10] it sees itself as being simply 'Canadian'. Unfortunately, that perception complicates matters. The dominant group, having an overarching pan-state identity, tends to perceive other ethnic groups, even those that are 'separate', as if they are 'embedded'; and inversely, the Québécois tend to see the 'overarching' Canadians as if they are 'separate'.

The introduction of the option 'Canadian' in the survey has another significant effect, unexpected by its magnitude. Only 13 per cent of respondents describe themselves as hyphenated Canadians and only 4 per cent identify with a foreign nation.[11] For a country of large immigration, these statistics measure a remarkable success at integrating and assimilating newcomers, but they measure also the serious failure, already noted, in obtaining the allegiance of a large number of Québécois.

Conclusion

The picture given by Table 3, though more satisfying than that of Table 2, still lacks refinement. The populations we allocated to different cells are in fact lined up along a continuum that runs from 'pure pan-state' to 'strong separatist'. In the case of the 'embedded' category, we lack measures of psychological distance between and among the identities linked to one another; and, as already mentioned, we suspect that, for a fair number of individuals, a Canadian second-order identity should be added to what our data led us to describe simply as 'separate'. The surveys done on the occasion of the Québec referendum on sovereignty, which was held at the time of publication (30 October 1995), enable us to take a better reading of the relative importance of our different types of ethnic and citizenship identifications. It is unlikely however that the more refined picture emerging from these surveys will depart markedly from that presented by Table 3, except in reducing the number of individuals we assigned to the 'separate' category, especially outside Québec. But even after such adjustments, Canada will retain the dominant characteristic emerging from the attitudinal data, that of a state that absorbs easily its incoming immigration but keeps bumping against its colonial past. Citizenship strongly binds the newcomers, but binds only weakly many of the descendants of the conquered communities, even when the conquest has been largely forgotten (for example, the Québécois, if not the Natives). Canada combines features of the United States where citizenship binds strongly many different embedded ethnicities, and features of Belgium where citizenship is a weak link between separate nations. Canada is thus an excellent example of a country where ethnicity generates citizenship, and where, inversely, citizenship generates ethnicity.

The importance of the second of these two processes – citizenship generating ethnicity – offers an argument for adding to the usual criteria of ethnic differences – race, religion, language, national origin, and territory – the specific criterion of citizenship. Would adding that criterion signify the rejection of primordialism for countries such as Canada where citizenship is within such easy reach of the newcomers? Not necessarily. A change of citizenship, like a change of religion, can provide an instant link to a new distant past, real or imaginary. Citizenship, like religion, can offer instant primordialism.

NOTES

1. G. Ferrero, *Pouvoir: les génies invisibles dans la cité* (New York: Brentano's, 1942).
2. For an introduction to the debate see James G. Kellas, *The Politics of Nationalism and Ethnicity* (London: Macmillan, 1991).
3. For references to the literature on immigration, see E. Tepper, 'Immigration Policy and Multiculturalism' in J.W. Berry and J.A. Laponce, *Ethnicity and Culture in Canada: the Research Landscape* (Toronto University Press) pp.95–123.
4. In 1994, for the first time since asking the question in 1988, *Ekos Surveys* found that a majority of Canadians (53 per cent) thought that there were too many immigrants (only 30 per cent said so in 1988). This finding may explain in part the reduction of the immigration target for 1995 to less than 200,000. But Canada needs migrants to replace a dying population. Its rate of reproduction is negative for both Anglophones and Francophones. The Aboriginals, by contrast, have a high rate of 3.5 comparable to that of third world countries, but they account for only 3 per cent to 4 per cent of the population. For public discussions of Canada's immigration policy see *The Globe and Mail*, March 10, 1994; and *La Presse*, October 6, 1994.
5. Walker Connor, 'A nation is a nation, is a state, is an ethnic group, is a . . .' *Ethnic and Racial Studies*, 1 (1978) pp.377–4009
6. A more detailed model would distinguish further the cases of 'separate but equal' identities that one uses like distinct currencies, according to roles and circumstances. See Jean Tournon, 'Construction et déconstruction du groupe ethnique', *International Political Science Review*, Vol. 10 (1989), pp.331–348.
7. The separate category includes separatists but is not to be equated with it. One can have a separate identity without being a separatist.
8. For a study of the membership rules of Indian bands, see Stewart Clatworthy and Anthony Smith, *Populations Implications of the 1985 Amendment to the Indian Act* (Perth, Ontario Living Dimensions, 1992).
9. John George Durham, *The Report on the Affairs of British North America* (Toronto: Stanton, 1839); André Siegfried, *Le Canada, les deux races: problèmes politiques contemporains* (Paris: Colin, 1906).
10. A linguistic dominant group may be no more aware of its language than a righthander is aware of being right-handed.
11. J.W. Berry and R. Kalin, 'Multicultural and Ethnic Attitudes in Canada' (paper read at the Montreal meeting of the Canadian Psychology Association, 1993). For variations in the rate of retention of 'ethnic' languages and ethnic social interactions in Toronto see Raymond Breton *et al.*, *Ethnic Identity and Equality* (Toronto University Press, 1990).

Full Partnership in the Fortunes and in the Future of the Nation

ROBERT CRAIG BROWN

The relationship of citizenship to ethnicity in Canada has seldom been studied by scholars. This paper traces the history of the concept of citizenship, and its relation to ethnicity, as Canada evolved from a colony at Confederation (1867) to autonomous nationhood (post 1931). The development of subjectship/citizenship legislation; its linkage to ethnic selectivity in immigration policy and restrictions on the full exercise of the rights of citizenship by some ethnic groups in Canada are the themes of the analysis from the 1860s to the 1980s.

The title of this paper is taken from the words of the Hon. Paul Martin, Secretary of State in the Mackenzie King Government, when he introduced his Canadian Citizenship Bill on 20 March, 1946. For him it was a most important occasion, his contribution to the sense of unity and common purpose among Canadians that characterized the days immediately following World War II. Canada had emerged from the war victorious, powerful and confident, and Martin believed that it was 'of the utmost importance that all of us, new Canadian and old, have a consciousness of a common purpose and common interests as Canadians.'[1] Citizenship, Martin went on to say,

> means more than the right to vote; more than the right to hold and
> transfer property, more than the right to move freely under the
> protection of the state; citizenship is the right to full partnership in the
> fortunes and in the future of the nation.[2]

In that same year, 1946, Canada's eighth decade as a Dominion in the British Empire Commonwealth was coming to a close. From the first years of contact between European adventurers and Canada's Amerindian peoples, long before Confederation, the territory that became the Dominion of Canada had been a land of immigrants, of people from away who came here to seek their fortune, and upon whom the land depended for its fortune. In the four generations between the establishment of the Dominion and Martin's speech, just short of six and one half million people[3] had entered Canada as immigrants.[4] Nearly all of them, it is fair to suggest, expected to achieve 'full partnership in the fortunes and in the future of the nation'...

How people from abroad could achieve that recognition of 'full partnership' with native born Canadians had been a matter of regular concern to both governments and legislatures. Significant changes in naturalization legislation had occupied the attention of Canada's Parliament on several occasions prior to the introduction of Martin's Bill.

In 1868 Parliament enacted legislation conferring naturalization on all people who had been naturalized in the confederating provinces.[5] The process of naturalization of an alien ('One born in a strange country, under the obedience of a strange prince or country')[6] was governed by Imperial Statutes, The Naturalization Acts, 1870 and 1872. It was not until 1881 that the Government of Canada introduced and passed The Naturalization Act, Canada, 1881, to provide, in the words of a contemporary learned commentator, 'a simple and inexpensive method of naturalization applicable to the whole Dominion and opening wide the door of British citizenship to persons of foreign birth who come to settle in Canada, without at the same time, requiring them to abjure the country of their nativity.'[7] The point at issue in the 1881 Act was captured in the commentator's last phrase, that is to say, that a prior claim of citizenship by the state in which an alien was born could not hinder the alien's right to seek, and be granted, under specific conditions, naturalization as a British subject in Canada.

In the same Act aliens were confirmed in their rights to the same capacities with regard to holding real estate as British subjects.[8] The alien was required to be a resident of Canada for at least three years and to certify the intent, when naturalized, to reside in Canada or to serve under the Government of Canada or one of its Provinces. The alien would be entitled to 'all political and other rights, powers and privileges, and be subject to all obligations, to which a natural born British subject is entitled or subject within Canada.' If abroad in the state from which he emigrated, he would not be deemed to be a British subject unless he had formally ceased to be a subject of the state of his birth. Aliens in the Dominion to whom the Act did not apply, that is to say those who could not be accorded naturalization, were persons classified as 'infant, lunatic, idiot, or married woman'[9] The last exclusion is particularly noteworthy: women who were married to aliens, including women born as British subjects, were deemed to hold the citizenship/subjectship of their husbands, and that provision was not removed from Canadian naturalization law until the passage of Martin's bill in 1946.[10]

In 1914 the Borden Government introduced a new Naturalization Bill which extended the time of residence for aliens from three to five year before acquiring status as a British subject. The Bill resulted from an agreement at the Imperial Conference of 1911 to have a uniform residence requirement throughout the Empire and provided that four of the five years could be passed in any part of the Empire; but the last year had to be spent in the country of intended residence. The 1914 Act also removed a distinction between native born and naturalized subjects where, before 1914, naturalized British subjects in Canada had not had their naturalization recognized outside of Canada.[11] In 1921, during the brief time of the Meighen Government, a Canadian Nationals Act was passed which made minor changes to Canada's naturalization legislation to bring it into conformity with Canadian commitments to the League of Nations.[12] And there matters stood until Martin's Bill was passed in 1946.

The Conservative historian, Donald Creighton, years later described the Canadian Citizenship Act of 1946 as a 'radical measure which brought about a fundamental change in the status of Canadians.' Up until then, he explained,

> British nationality, or British 'subjecthood', had been the basic identity of all peoples under the British Crown; and Canadian citizenship, in so far as it existed at all, was simply a minor local variation. The Canadian act completely reversed this order. It made Canadian citizenship primary and basic, and British nationality secondary and derivative; 'a Canadian citizen is a British subject', the act declared briefly....This virtually forced Great Britain and the other Dominions to adopt the new Canadian principles, and in 1948 the British passed an act which for the first time defined the 'citizenship of the United Kingdom'.[13]

Martin certainly intended that the 1946 Act bring about a major change and he, himself, would have gone further. He had wanted to leave out the section of his Bill which allowed Canadians to remain British subjects. 'It left Canada with a mark of inferiority,' he later recalled.[14] But he could not persuade his Cabinet colleagues to make such a decisive break with tradition. Still, the 1946 Act was a landmark in Canada's naturalization legislation. Naturalized Canadians, non-Canadian British subjects who had lived in Canada for five years and non-Canadian women who had married Canadians and lived in Canada would become citizens forthwith. The Act also changed the condition for citizenship from a knowledge of French or English to proof of twenty years of residence. This allowed many long time residents of Canada from Eastern Europe to become citizens. And the act did away with the inferior status of women married to naturalized subjects/citizens, which the constitutional scholar W.P.M. Kennedy had recommended be removed as early as 1930,[15] was done.

A number of distinctions regarding ethnic origin, sex, residence requirements and marital status remained in the 1946 Canadian Citizenship Act. In 1976 another Citizenship Act was passed which eliminated the privileged status of British subjects and required that all applicants for citizenship, of whatever ethnic origin and of either sex, be treated equally. In addition the residence requirement was reduced from five to three years and the age of majority was reduced from twenty-one to eighteen years.[16]

Canada's naturalization legislation since Confederation, apart from the provisions relating to infants, lunatics, idiots and women married to aliens, gives few clues as to who can be admitted through the gateway to 'full partnership' in the nation. The assumption in each of the Acts prior to 1976 was that all those who are allowed to enter Canada for purpose of permanent residence would, in due course, become subjects/citizens. Well, not quite all, as we shall see in a moment. The issue of who can enter Canada with the intention of becoming a subject/citizen, and the conditions upon which those people are eligible for entry, have not been defined in the Naturalization Acts. Instead, these very important matters are spelled out in the various Acts of Parliament and in regulations imposed by Order-in-Council since Confederation.[17]

Immigration is a shared responsibility between the central and the provincial governments. Throughout most of our history it has been the central government which has taken the initiative in seeking to attract immigrants to Canada. But in the early years even its initiatives were slight and sporadic. A 1974 report on immigration for the Department of Manpower and Immigration characterized the first three decades in policy terms as the 'free entry period'.[18] By 1896 just under one and a half million immigrants had been admitted to Canada. Apart from some sporadic encouragement of immigration from Britain by Canadian High Commissioners after 1880, most migrants had come on their own or at the initiative of railway companies, especially the Canadian Pacific, which became, in effect, Canada's primary immigration agent abroad. With government encouragement the railways tended to concentrate their effort on Britain and, to some extent, on Northern Europe. In addition, there was a steady supply throughout most of these years of immigrants from the United States. The Government was ready to assist trans-Atlantic migrants by paying part of the transportation costs and to provide all settlers with cheap or free land in western Canada. Regulations defining categories not to be admitted were few, mainly directed at criminals and other 'vicious classes' (1872) and paupers and destitute immigrants (1879).

There was one significant exception to this 'free entry' phase: migration to Canada of people of Chinese origin. Since its entry into Confederation British Columbia had attempted to bar Chinese from entry into the province but its own legislative acts were consistently disallowed by Ottawa. Finally, in response to pressure from the province and its MPs, Sir John A. Macdonald's Government established a Royal Commission on Chinese

Immigration in 1884. The next year the government passed the Chinese Immigration Act 'to restrict and regulate Chinese immigration'.[19] The Act imposed a stiff head tax of $50 on each Chinese migrant (diplomats, tourists, merchants, men of science and students were excepted) and other restrictions were designed to sharply curb, if not eliminate, immigration to Canada of people of Chinese origin. It is worth adding that, as the 1974 Report observed, 'other non-white immigrants, notably ex-slaves from the United States, were not subjected to restriction.'[20]

The emphasis in government policy in the early years, such as it was, was to attract farmers. It was generally assumed that most newcomers would be of good, hard working, dependable Anglo-Saxon or Northern and Western European stock. As a development policy – and immigration policy was a development policy[21] – this was just what the Government of Canada desired. Such peoples were assumed to share similar political values and to be able to 'fit in' to Canadian society. But the policy failed to achieve the result expected by the government. Development of the territories of the West scarcely happened, in part because of hard times, in part because the government did not force railways to choose the acreage of their land grants which left vast tracts of land inaccessible to settlement, and in part because emigration from Canada in the late nineteenth century nearly matched immigration to Canada from all sources. Between 1871 and 1891 an estimated 1,549,000 Canadians left Canada, most to seek their fortunes in the United States.[22]

At the turn of the century vastly improved economic conditions in Canada and abroad, a new government in Canada, extensive new investment in the Canadian economy and a new and vigorous interest in immigration policy by the government produced dramatic changes in policy and its implementation. In 1896, the year the Laurier Government was elected, only 16,835 migrants had entered Canada; by 1907 the number had climbed to 272,409 and in 1913 it had soared to 400,870[23] Preference was still given to farmers who had experience in dry-land farming. Thousands came from the United States (including many Canadians who had migrated there in earlier decades), Britain and Europe, especially Eastern Europe. A new priority in this period was for domestic servants, reflecting the demands of a rapidly growing middle class in Canada's cities. And though the government officially discouraged migration of urban workers and common labourers, they too came in the thousands to find employment in the growing network of factories in Eastern Canada, or in building the new transcontinental railways, or to work in forests and mines. Large numbers of these, usually single men, were 'sojourners' who intended to make money and return to their homelands. But larger numbers still were men who sought fortunes for themselves and their families in Canada. While most of the immigrants intended to settle in the west or Ontario, Quebec was putting together a colonization program to lure Quebeckers back from the United States to develop the forest and hydro-electric resources of that province.

These were heady, prosperous times. Between 1901 and 1921 there was a 64 percent growth in population from 5.37 million to 8.78 million people. An English observer in 1906 remarked that Canada was about to become 'the cornerstone of the temple of the British Empire' and in 1909 an immigration pamphlet proudly proclaimed that 'the United States is the America of achievement, but Canada is the America of opportunity.'[24]

Not all Canadians shared the optimism of the 'boomers'. Canada was changing: too much, too fast, some thought. The flood of newcomers brought strange voices, strange faces, strange customs. So much so that in 1909 J.S. Woodsworth and a journalistic colleague published a study of the migrant groups, *Strangers in the Land*, arranging them 'scientifically' according to their ability to fit in to Canadian society. Many many others, especially among the country's 'better elements', took a harsher view as they worried that Canada's values and traditions would be overwhelmed by the migrants. Henri Bourassa spoke for many in both English and French Canada when he pleaded that Canada not become 'a land of refuge for the scum of all nations'.[25] The clamour became so intense that the Minister of the Interior, Clifford Sifton, who had already made major changes in procedures relating to immigration, recognized that new measures needed to be taken.

Soon after he entered the Cabinet in 1897 Sifton centralized the administration of immigration in Ottawa. His Department (Interior) then initiated extensive and vigorous promotional campaigns to attract immigrants from the United States, Britain and Europe. Soon, as the voices of doubt and fear rose to a chorus of complaint, the Department began to use regulations under the Immigration Act to control the admission of immigrants and their welfare before and after entry into Canada. The 1974 report noted that, in addition to Sifton's reputation for aggressive promotion of immigration. He deserves to be just as well known as the founder of the concept of selective immigration. His activities created an approach that remains the foundation of policy and law to this day.[26] Under his direction the head tax on Chinese migrants was increased to $100 in 1900 and raised again in 1903 to the almost prohibitive level of $500. In 1902 'diseased persons' were added to the list of classes of people to be refused admittance to Canada.

Frank Oliver, who succeeded Sifton as Minister of Interior in 1905, was a strong advocate of strictly controlled immigration. He carried the process of selectivity much further. A 1906 amendment to the Immigration Act provided that the Department could make regulations 'necessary or expedient for the carrying out of this Act according to its true intent and meaning and for the better attainment of its objectives.' This sweeping power was used in 1908 to exclude charity dependent migrants and to require 'landing money' ($25 in Summer and $50 in Winter) from most migrants, though farm labourers, domestic servants and certain relatives of newcomers in Canada were excluded from this requirement.

Both Sifton and Oliver would have liked to impose a head tax on Japanese migrants but Britain's diplomatic alliance with Japan prevented it. Following the anti-oriental riots in Vancouver in 1907, a Canadian mission to Tokyo led to the agreement by the government of Japan to sharply limit migration of Japanese nationals to Canada. An Order-in-Council in the same year forbade entrance of Asian immigrants who did not come to Canada by direct continuous journey from their homeland. Another regulation imposed a charge of $200 landing money on all Asiatic migrants other than Japanese and Chinese. Together, these measures effectively barred migration to Canada by fellow British subjects from India and led to the Komagata Maru incident in 1914 in Vancouver harbour. In 1910–1911, under pressure from Albertans, the Department used its selection power to prevent entry of about 1000 blacks from Oklahoma. After further changes to the Immigration Act in 1910 the Deputy Minister proudly reported that the policy of the Department was to do 'all in its power to keep out of the country undesirables' in three classes: migrants who were physically, mentally or morally unfit; 'those belonging to nationalities unlikely to assimilate and who consequently prevent the building up of a united nation of people of similar customs and ideals;' and 'those who from their mode of life and occupation are likely to crowd into urban centres and bring about a state of congestion which might result in unemployment and a lowering of the standard of our national life.'[27]

By 1919 the list of prohibited classes of migrants had grown to a lengthy catalogue. In that year, in the aftermath of the Great War, the Russian Revolution and the Winnipeg General Strike, harsh new amendments were added to the Immigration Act. Non-citizens and naturalized subjects who were deemed to advocate or associate with advocates of the overthrow of constituted authority could be deported, and any person who had been deported from an allied country as a 'radical' could be barred from Canada. Primary targets of these changes, and of surveillance by the RCMP, were Ukrainian, Russian, Finnish and Jewish immigrants.[28] A year earlier enemy aliens, labourers destined for British Columbia, and Mennonites, Doukhobors and Hutterites were barred from entry and the landing money requirement was raised to $250.[29] In 1922 the restriction on Mennonites and Hutterites was withdrawn as it was for Doukhobors in 1926. In the same year a new Chinese Immigration Act cut off migration from China completely. For a brief time in the interwar period, 1926 to 1930, immigration levels exceeded more than 100 thousand per annum, then plummeted to new lows in the Depression. A record low 7576 immigrants were admitted to Canada in 1942 in the middle of the second world war. Paul Martin's Citizenship Act coincided with a return to increasing levels of immigration to Canada. The annual rates never reached the record highs of 1910 to 1913, but for most years in the 1950s, 1960s, 1970s and 1980s were high. Between 1947 and 1987 more than 5.5 million migrants were admitted to Canada. Mackenzie King announced in 1947 that immigration policy would continue to be highly selective. Doubtless he was trying to reassure nervous Canadians that they would not be flooded with waves of migrants and refugees. But King soon retired and the major characteristic of immigration policy since World War II has been to liberalize, gradually, the process of selectivity. To meet Canada's obligations under the United Nations Charter the Chinese Immigration Act was repealed in 1947 and Chinese immigration was allowed under the sponsored 'family class' of permitted migrants. The 'continuous journey' regulation was also rescinded in the immediate post war years and in 1950 Germans who qualified as sponsored immigrants were removed from the enemy alien restrictions list. By then a distinction between sponsored and independent migrants was firmly in place. The Minister continued to have strong discretionary authority and priority was given to sponsored immigrants, to agriculturalists, professionals, businessmen and domestics in the independent class and to certain classes of workers. Blacks were not admissible unless they qualified in one of the preferred classes or were immediate relatives of Canadian residents.[30]

Cautious liberalization and the results of giving priority status to sponsored immigrants led to some unanticipated results. Reg Whitaker noted that the 'family class' category encouraged the entry of more workers with low skills, and 'the expansion of ethnic groups already established in Canada with strong kinship ties ... it helped foster, especially in major cities, strong ethnic pressure groups with political leverage.'[31] Many of the old fears and shibboleths of the 1900s were rekindled in the late 1950s and early 1960s. One remarkable example was expressed by the Moderator of the United Church of Canada in 1962. The Very Reverend Hugh McLeod viewed immigration policy as being determined 'to make Canada predominantly Roman Catholic'.

> Perhaps Roman Catholics have been the only eligible immigrants available in large numbers, and as people they are doubtless estimable and capable of greatly enriching our nation, but as members of a

Church which everywhere favors the establishment of a monolithic infallible authority under Rome, they may herald and achieve the end of liberty as we have known it and as we deem it necessary for life.[32]

A White Paper in 1966, and a review by a special Parliamentary Committee, led to dramatic changes in immigration regulations in 1967. Most important was the elimination of discrimination on the basis of race or nationality. A point system based on education and training, need for occupation in Canada, knowledge of English or French, and the like was introduced for independent immigrants. And the qualifications for 'family class' immigrants were tightened. In the years that followed the pattern of immigration also changed, away from Europe and towards Asia and other Third World areas.

In 1978 a new Immigration Law consolidated most of the policy changes of previous years. Its purpose, *inter alia*, was to promote demographic goals established by the government of Canada; to enrich the social and cultural fabric of Canada, to ensure non-discrimination by race, nationality, religion, colour or sex and to fulfil Canada's obligations to refugees. These principals established, the core of immigration policy since Sifton's day remained intact. Legal scholar Julius Gray observed that the 1978 Act's 'main thrust was to confirm the restrictions that had been the hallmark of immigration law since at least 1910.'[33]

Looking back, it is clear that a process of selectivity which determined who would be eligible for 'full partnership' in Canada has been in place since Confederation. In the 'free entry' period selectivity was largely circumstantial and could be taken for granted in the legislative and regulative process. Depression, hard times, the slow development of transportation facilities and a lax administration of land grants throughout the period effectively curtailed immigration from sources other than the United Kingdom and the United States in most years before the turn of the century. The government's own efforts at promotion of immigration were confined to the United Kingdom. The need for cheap contract labour to build the Pacific railway and to exploit the mining resources on Vancouver Island did promote, with Ottawa's off-and-on support until 1885, migration of Chinese labourers to British Columbia. But strong opposition there forced the passage of the first Chinese Immigration Act in that year.

Better times, better transportation facilities and more efficient management of the alienation of public lands opened Canada's doorways just as the new century began. The government itself turned to aggressive promotion of immigration in the United States, Britain and Europe. At the same time, a regime of increasingly systematic regulatory acts defined ever more classes of prohibited people on the basis of physical, mental and moral fitness, personal character, race and nationality. After each of the World Wars 'political correctness' was added to the list of prohibited classes; 'radicals' at the end of the First War and Communists after the Second. Only in the last generation and a half have the barriers of race and nationality, religion and sex been eliminated. Still the principle of selectivity remains, especially for independent, as distinct from 'family class' immigrants, and point systems and other controls have tended in recent years to favour some groups and some classes of people over others aspiring for 'full partnership' in Canada's fortune and future.

Controlling the Franchise

For most Canadians the most tangible benefit of citizenship is the right to vote. Interestingly, until very recent times, Canada's governments and Parliaments have been as selective in granting the right to vote as they have been in controlling immigration. At Confederation the new government of Canada adopted the existing provincial franchises as the federal franchise. The provinces already had selective qualifications firmly established. Two restrictions were generally applied: suffrage was confined to adult male British subjects and each subject had to meet a property qualification, generally speaking $300 in real property in cities and towns and $200 in rural areas. Some of the provinces excluded Indians from the franchise, even though they were British subjects. In British Columbia the Chinese were disfranchised in the very first session of the new post-Confederation legislature.[34]

In 1885 Sir John A. Macdonald brought in a Bill establishing a separate franchise for federal elections. Property qualifications were continued and a $400 income qualification, which did not apply to wage earners, was added. Macdonald also proposed to enfranchise widows and spinsters and Indians who met the property qualification. Macdonald argued that unmarried women who possessed property 'who have the responsibilities consequent on having property, [should] have the right of protecting that property by giving them votes'[35] but his proposal was quickly disposed of in committee. The debate on enfranchisement of some Indians occupied the House of Commons attention for several weeks. Eventually Parliament accepted enfranchisement of most Indians in Eastern Canada who held property, and no franchise for Indians in Western Canada, who were regarded as wards of the state. Macdonald's explanations for the distinction are worth recalling. 'We are actuated,' he remarked, 'by the same desire to give British subjects, red or white, if they have the property qualification, the right to vote.' The Bill was designed to give a vote 'to those Indians who have the ostensible evidences of property which the white man can show.' Drawing a distinction between Indians in Eastern and Western Canada, Macdonald said the former 'carry out all the obligations of civilized men' while the latter 'are not ready for the franchise'.[36]

The other significant application of selectivity in the first federal franchise act was to exclude 'Chinese and Mongolians', a concession, like the Chinese Immigration Act of the same year, to British Columbia. Explaining this clause, Macdonald compared his views of Indians and Chinese.

> ...Indians are sons of the soil; they are Canadians and British subjects; and, therefore, if they have the property qualification, I think they ought to be treated as other British subjects. The Chinese are foreigners. If they come to this country, after three years residence, they may, if they choose, be naturalized. But still we know that when the Chinaman comes here he intends to return to his own country; he does not bring his family with him; he is a stranger, a sojourner in a strange land, for his own purposes for a while; he has no common interest with us, and while he gives us his labour and is paid for it, and is valuable ... a Chinaman gives us his labour and gets his money, but that money does not fructify in Canada; he does not invest it here, but he takes it with him and returns to China... he has no British instincts or British feelings or aspirations, and therefore ought not to have a vote. [37]

In 1898 the recently elected Liberal Government returned control of the franchise for federal elections to the provinces. By then only two provinces, Nova Scotia and Quebec, continued to have property qualifications for enfranchisement. Though the Prime Minister, Wilfrid Laurier, stated his personal opposition to the principle, the Franchise Act of 1898 provoked little opposition to manhood suffrage. As the late Norman Ward remarked in his standard study of the issue, 'some time between 1885 and 1898 the notion that the franchise was a trust accompanying property, rather than a right normally accompanying citizenship, all but disappeared in federal politics.'[38] The 1898 Franchise Act continued the existing exclusions of Indians and Inuit and Chinese from the franchise where such prohibitions were present in provincial laws. In British Columbia the exclusions went further. Japanese were deprived of the franchise in the province in 1895 and East Indians in 1907.[39]

The most extraordinary manipulation of the franchise in our history occurred in 1917 when the Borden Government, facing a war-time election, deliberately and outrageously 'fixed' the franchise to help guarantee its success at the polls in Canada and on the battlefields of Europe. Two Acts were involved of which the more significant was the Wartime Elections Act.

The Act summarily disfranchised Canadians from enemy countries who had been naturalized after 31 March, 1902 (that is, those naturalized Canadians who had immigrated since 1899) as well as Mennonites, Hutterites and Doukhobors and conscientious objectors. It enfranchised women whose husbands, sons, brothers or fathers were serving in the Canadian Expeditionary Force and men whose sons or grandsons were serving in the CEF. The Military Voters Act extended the franchise to all service personnel, whether citizens or not, serving in either the Canadian or British forces , including minors or Indians. The greatest impact, calculated by the government, was in western Canada. Ward noted that in Humboldt constituency, for example, the number of eligible electors in one poll dropped from 182 to 22 and in another from 63 to one. A year later the new Union Government introduced a new national franchise for federal elections which included an extension of the franchise to women. In 1920 the same government again disfranchised Canadians of Asian origin by providing that people who have been disfranchised in any province because of race, unless they were war veterans, were disqualified from voting in federal elections. In the same year the franchise was restored to the peoples disfranchised in 1917.[40]

In World War II the Liberal Government, in general, refrained from the sweeping gerrymandering that took place in the earlier war, except for the denial of the right of Japanese Canadians to vote (as in British Columbia and Saskatchewan by the 1920 legislation). In 1944 it introduced legislation, retroactive to 1938, disfranchising all persons disqualified by race in provincial laws, the effect of which was to disfranchise, for example, Japanese Canadians who, since 1938, had moved from British Columbia to a province like Ontario. In 1947 the provincial and federal disfranchisement of Chinese and East Indians came to an end and the same happened for Japanese Canadians in 1948 and 1949.[41] The franchise was extended to the Inuit in 1950 but it was not given to status Indians until 1960.

The fevered temperaments of wartime, especially in the Great War, drove Canadians, especially Canadians of British origin, to demand that some Canadians, those who came here from 'enemy' countries and those who by religious conviction were pacifists, be deprived of the right of citizens to vote. More significantly, provinces and federal governments alike, for nearly a century after Confederation, in peace and in war, deprived other British subjects and Canadian citizens of Asian or native origin of a fundament aspect of 'full partnership' in the fortunes and future of Canada.

The intense nationalistic prejudices of wartime divided Canadians against each other in other ways as well. At the beginning of the Great War there were more than 400,000 immigrants of German origin (more than half Canadian born) and about 120,000 Austro-Hungarians in Canada, most of the latter in fact Ukrainians from Galacia and Bukovyna. Only those not yet naturalized, about 20,000 Germans and 60,000 Ukrainians, were 'enemy aliens'. Initially both the British Government and alarmed British Canadians put intense pressure upon the Borden Government to intern all of these people. Only 8,579 were actually interned: about 1400 prisoners of war; some 1200 Germans and 5954 'Austrians', all but a few hundred of whom were Ukrainians. It is reasonable to assume that nearly all the internees, save for the actual prisoners of war were, if not yet naturalized, intending to become Canadians. Most of the internees were released by mid-war but the suspicion of Germans, Austro-Hungarians and, after 1917, Russians and Finns, remained intense. In the autumn of 1918 papers published in German, Ukrainian and seven other 'enemy alien' languages were banned as were meetings conducted in the language of an 'enemy' country or Russia, Ukraine or Finland. Numerous left-wing political organizations were similarly banned and their adherents could be arrested without warrant and imprisoned. All of these measures of the Union Government were directed at Canadian citizens – 'doubtful British' as they were sometimes called.[42]

Some of the same groups of people, and others, found themselves only hesitantly welcomed or denied when they attempted to join the Canadian Expeditionary Force. Those most frequently mentioned in historical accounts were French Canadians.[43] With few exceptions, such as the 22nd Regiment, French Canadians largely found themselves 'strangers' in the unilingual (English) Canadian Expeditionary Force. And, especially during Sam Hughes' tenure as Minister of Militia and Defence (to 1916), efforts to recruit French Canadians were continuously clouded by suspicions of bias. Racial bias was certainly evident in the refusal of an offer of Japanese Canadians to form a battalion (Japan was an ally of the British in the Great War) though individual volunteers were accepted. In the end 194 Japanese Canadians served in the CEF. Though some Blacks served in front line battalions most were segregated into the 2nd Canadian Construction Company.[44] Indians, stereotyped as 'ferocious fighting men', were welcomed into the forces and were heavily recruited, especially in Ontario where the Six Nations Indians demanded that the request to serve come from the King, not the Canadian government. Indians who did serve were, as noted above, given the franchise. After the passage of the Military Service Act there was some question whether those Indians who did not enjoy the full rights of citizenship could be conscripted and eventually, in January, 1918, an Order-in-Council exempted all Indians from compulsory service.[45] Among European immigrant groups, some 10,000 naturalized Canadians served in the War[46] but, more generally, offers to raise battalions of naturalized Canadians from central and eastern Europe were not encouraged. On the other hand, attempts to raise English, Scottish and Irish battalions were enthusiastically supported by the Militia Department.

In World War II the pattern of selectivity by race and national origin which characterized recruitment in the Great War was less evident, in large part because of a different and much more centralized method of recruiting.[47] By then over 90 percent of the Japanese Canadians were citizens and many served in the war, as did nearly 35,000 Ukrainians and countless representatives of other minority communities. The Government of Canada urged Mennonites and Hutterites, both of which groups had received exemption from military service as a condition of settlement, to accept alternative service; some Mennonites accepted and the Hutterites adamantly refused.[48]

In World War II all Germans who had been naturalized since 1922 were required to register with the Canadian government and some 1200 were interned. The 'enemy alien' classification also included all Italian Canadians who had been naturalized after 1929 and, of 700 who were interned, more than 200 were naturalized citizens and twenty were native born.[49] The harshest treatment of either war was directed at Japanese Canadians in World War II. In 1941 there were just over 22,000 people of Japanese origin in Canada; nearly 17,000 were Canadian born and another 3,288 had been naturalized.[50] On December 8, 1941, the Royal Canadian Navy seized their fishing boats. Ten days later all Japanese Canadians, regardless of place of birth, were required to register with the government and at the end of February all who lived within 100 miles of the Pacific Coast were evacuated and their property was seized and placed under the protection of a 'Custodian of Japanese Property'. The property was suddenly sold in January, 1943 and, at the end of the war, the government issued deportation orders for Japanese Canadians. Though the courts did not uphold the orders, about one-sixth of them left for Japan. Those who remained in Canada were not allowed to return to the coast but were dispersed to the east.[51]

Conclusion

From 1867 until very recent times governments and Parliaments of Canada have imbedded principles of selectivity in legislation, administrative procedure and policy to determine who might and who might not enjoy the right of 'full partnership' in the nation's fortune and future. Even among our indigenous peoples a discriminatory policy was applied against Indians and Inuit and Canadian born and naturalized Canadians of Asian origin in exercising their right to vote until the post World War II era. But most of our legislative acts and administrative processes have been directed at discriminating among who could and who could not enter Canada from abroad for purposes of residence. White people from other parts of the Empire/Commonwealth and from the United States have always enjoyed a priority status in discriminatory policies and procedures. Until very recently people of Asian or African racial or national origin have either been excluded or strongly discouraged from seeking their own fortunes in Canada. Explicit barriers based on race and nationality, creed and sex have been removed since the Second World War, but selectivity remains in place. The tightening of definitions of admissible people in the 'family class' and of qualifications for independent migrants continues, to this day, to make it easier for some people gain entrance to Canada than others.

NOTES

1.   Paul Martin, 'Citizenship and the People's World' in William Kaplan, ed., *Belonging: The Meaning and Future of Canadian Citizenship* (Montreal and Kingston: McGill-Queen's University Press, 1993) p.70
2.   Ibid. p.73.
3.   On the reliability of immigration statistics prior to the 1920's see M. C. Urquhart and K. A. H. Buckley, *Historical Statistics of Canada* (Toronto, Macmillan, 1965), pp.9–13. All figures used in this paper should be regarded as estimates, especially for the years before the 1920's.
4.   Calculated from Table 1 in Reg Whitaker, *Canadian Immigration Policy Since Confederation.* (Ottawa, Canadian Historical Association), p.2.
5.   William Kaplan, 'The Evolution of Citizenship Legislation in Canada'. (Canada, Multiculturalism and Citizenship Canada,1991), p.11.
6.   Alfred Howell, *Naturalization and Nationality in Canada* (Toronto, Carswell & Co., 1884) p.5.
7.   Kaplan. 'Evolution of Citizenship', p.11. Howell, p.3.
8.   On the distinctions between subjectship and citizenship see Robert Bothwell, 'Something of Value? Subjects and Citizens in Canadian History' in Kaplan, *Belonging,* 1993, pp.26–35.
9.   Howell, p.46.
10. Martin, p.69. Martin went on to observe that Canada thus was the first nation in the Commonwealth to recognize 'the separate and independent status of women' with regard to the right of a wife to choose her citizenship.
11. J. C. Hopkins, *The Canadian Annual Review of Public Affairs, 1914* (Toronto, Annual Review Publishing Company, 1915), p.753.
12. Martin, p.67.
13. Donald Creighton, *The Forked Road. Canada, 1939–1957.* (Toronto, McClelland and Stewart, 1976), p.129.
14. Martin,p.74.
15. W. P.M. Kennedy, *Report submitted to the Honourable The Secretary of State for Canada on Some Problems in the Law of Nationality.* (Ottawa, Kings Printer, 1930), pp.25–32.
16. Kaplan, 'Evolution of Citizenship'. pp.22–27.
17. See William Kaplan, 'Who Belongs? Changing Concepts of Citizenship and Nationality' in Kaplan, *Belonging,* 1993, pp.243–64, for a comparative analysis over time of Canadian and other views on who is entitled to citizenship.
18. Canada, Manpower and Immigration, *Report of the Canadian Immigration and Population Study: 2. The immigration program.* (Ottawa, Information Canada, 1974), p.3.
19. Canada, *The immigration program.* p.5. See also Peter Ward, *White Canada Forever.*

Popular Attitudes and Public Policy Toward Orientals in British Columbia. (Montreal and Kingston, McGill-Queen's University Press, 1978), pp.38–42.
20. Ibid. p.5.
21. On immigration as a development policy see Whitaker,pp.3–6.
22. Urquhart and Buckley,Series B100–107, p.44.
23. Whitaker,Table 1, p.2.
24. Robert Craig Brown and Ramsay Cook, *Canada, 1896–1921. The Nation Transformed.* (Toronto, McClelland and Stewart, 1974), pp.49–50.
25. Cited, Robert Craig Brown, *Robert Laird Borden. A Biography, 1854–1914. Vol 1.* (Toronto, Macmillan, 1975), p.96.
26. Canada, *The immigration program,* p.6.
27. Ibid. pp.7–11. On the exclusion of the blacks from Oklahoma see Howard Palmer, *Patterns of Prejudice. A History of Nativism in Alberta.* (Toronto, McClelland and Stewart, 1982), pp.35–36. On the Komagata Maru incident see Ward, *White Canada Forever,* pp.88–93. 30. Ibid. pp.17–21.
28. Whitaker, p.11.
29. Canada, *The immigration program,* p.12.
31. Whitaker, p.16.
32. Cited, John Saywell, ed. , *The Canadian Annual Review for 1962.* (Toronto, University of Toronto Press, 1963) p.300.
33. Julius H. Gray, *Immigration Law in Canada.* (Toronto, Butterworths, 1984), p.13.
34. Norman Ward, *The Canadian House of Commons. Representation.* (Toronto, University of Toronto Press, 1963) Ward's book remains the standard authority on the subject. Thomas Hodgins, *The Canadian Franchise Act.* (Toronto, Rowsell & Hutchison, 1886) provided detailed commentary on the 1885 Franchise Act and provisions of the various contemporary provincial acts which it replaced for federal elections. On British Columbia see Ward, *White Canada Forever,* p.33.
35. Canada, Parliament, House of Commons, *Debates. 1885.* p.1389.
36. Ibid. pp.1487–88 and 1576.
37. Ibid. p.1582.
38. Ward, *House of Commons,* p.225.
39. Ward, *White Canada Forever,* p.180, note. 2.
40. Ward, *House of Commons,* pp.226–37. See also John Herd Thompson, *Ethnic Minorities During Two World Wars* (Ottawa, Canadian Historical Association, 1991), p.8.
41. Ward, *House of Commons,*p.236. Ward, *White Canada Forever,* p.165.
42. Thompson, pp.4–9. For more extended accounts see John Herd Thompson, *The Harvests of War. The Prairie West. 1914–1918* (Toronto, McClelland and Stewart, 1978), Chapter 4; Palmer, pp.47–60; Brown and Cook, Chapters 11 and 13; Joseph Boudreau, 'Western Canada's 'Enemy Aliens' in World War One', *Alberta Historical Review, Vol.12, No. 1,* Winter, 1964, pp.1–9 and Art Grenke, 'The German Community in Winnipeg and the English-Canadian Response to World War I', *Canadian Ethnic Studies, VOL. XX, No. 1,* 1958, pp.21–44. The standard account of the internment operation in World War I is in the last chapter of Desmond Morton, *The Canadian General: Sir William Otter.* (Toronto, Hakkert, 1974).
43. See Desmond Morton, *Canada and War. A Military and Political History.* (Toronto, Butterworths, 1981); Desmond Morton, *When Your Number's Up: The Canadian Soldier in the First World War.* (Toronto, Random House, 1993); J. L. Granatstein and J. M. Hitsman, *Broken Promises. A History of Conscription in Canada* (Toronto, Oxford, 1977); Ronald G. Haycock, *Sam Hughes. The Public Career of a Controversial Canadian.* (Waterloo, Wilfrid Laurier University Press, 1986); Brown and Cook, *Canada, 1896–1921;* and Robert Craig Brown, *Robert Laird Borden. A Biography, 1914–1937, Vol. 2.* (Toronto, Macmillan, 1980) among several accounts.
44. Morton, *Canada and War,* p.61 and Morton, *When Your Number's Up,* pp.57 and 291,note. 26.
45. Barbara Wilson, ed., *Ontario and the First World War, 1914–1918. A Collection of Documents.* (Toronto, Champlain Society, 1977) pp.cx–cxiv, 169–175. See also pp.cviii–cix,

166–168 for participation of Ontario Blacks in the war.
46. Thompson,*Ethnic Minorities*, p.6.
47. Granatstein and Hitsman, pp.135, 152–158; Morton, *Canada and War*, pp.105, 115–117, 137.
48. Thompson, *Ethnic Minorities*, pp.13–14.
49. Ibid. , pp.12–13. On German Canadians see Robert H. Keyserlingk, "Agents with the Gates": The Search for Nazi Subversives in Canada during World War II', *Canadian Historical Review*, Vol.1, No. 2, 1985, pp.211–239.
50. Ibid. p.15.
51. Ibid. pp.16–17. See also Ward, *White Canada Forever*, Chapter 8; Morton, *Canada and War*, p.110 and the essays by R. H. Keyserlingk, B. Ramirez and J. L. Granatstein and G. A. Johnson on German, Italian and Japanese Canadians in World War II in Norman Hillmer, *et al*, eds., *On Guard For Thee: War, Ethnicity and the Canadian State, 1939–1945*. (Ottawa, Canadian Committee for the History of the Second War, 1988).

Ethnicity and Citizenship Attitudes in Canada: Analyses of a 1991 National Survey

RUDOLF KALIN

The purpose of this article was to examine the citizenship attitudes of Canadians, specifically as these attitudes may vary by ethnic origin. Citizenship attitudes were operationalized in terms of having a Canadian (as opposed to a provincial or ethnic) identity and having a positive attachment to Canada. Results from a national survey with 3325 respondents conducted in 1991 by Angus Reid for Multiculturalism and Citizenship Canada were analyzed. Preference for a particular type of self-identity (Canadian, British-Canadian, French-Canadian, Provincial, Other Ethnic-Canadian, Other National) was assessed, as well as the rated strength of each of these identities. A scale measuring Canadianism, that is defined as an attachment to Canada was also used. Results showed that citizenship attitudes in Canada outside Québec are remarkably positive, with very few differences among respondents from various ethnic origins. In Québec, a distinctive pattern of attitudes reflecting Québec nationalism was found.

Introduction

Canada has been officially multicultural since 1971, when then Prime Minister Pierre Elliot Trudeau announced the multiculturalism policy in the House of Commons. The policy had several goals, among them the promotion of heritage retention by ethnic groups wishing to do so, and tolerance and acceptance of all groups. The policy was meant not to jeopardize national unity, but on the contrary, to promote it, by instilling 'confidence in one's own individual identity'. The architects of the policy believed heritage maintenance and national unity to be not only compatible, but in fact synergistic. The policy announcement in 1971 was followed by the Multiculturalism Act in 1988 which recognized the cultural and racial diversity of Canadian society and sought the freedom of all Canadians to 'preserve, enhance, and share their cultural heritage.'

While Canada has a multiculturalism policy, and while Canadians are undoubtedly from diverse ethnic origins, there is considerable discussion and debate about whether Canada is truly multicultural. Some of this debate pertains to terminology, particularly with regard to the precise meaning of 'ethnicity' and 'ethnic group' (Burnet, 1976, 1978, 1984; Isajiw, 1980; Li, 1990; Porter, 1980; Russell, 1994). Some consensus exists that 'ethnic group' refers to a group of people with a common heritage who share a common culture, language and religion, and who have a sense of identity. 'Ethnicity', or the state of being ethnic, although fraught with ambiguity, is nevertheless a useful term. It can refer to objective phenomena such as language, religion, practices and rituals, and so on. But it can also refer to psychological or symbolic aspects, such as a sense of identity. In addition to these qualitative aspects of ethnicity, there is also a quantitative dimension. Groups, as well as individuals, can have little or a lot of ethnicity.

The terms 'multicultural' and 'multiculturalism' have also been subject to discussion. Burnet (1975, 1978, 1984) has raised doubts regarding the feasibility of multiculturalism in Canada in the sense of having many full-fledged cultures developed and survive. Porter (1980) has raised doubts about the wisdom of emphasizing multiculturalism. Different meanings of ethnicity are inherent in the insightful discussion of multiculturalism (institutionalized, ritualistic, and symbolic) provided by Roberts and Clifton (1990). In 'institutionalized multiculturalism' ethnic groups have a relatively high level of institutional completeness (Breton, 1964). Members have a strong sense of identity and they conform to cultural norms and traditions. In 'ritualistic multiculturalism' members conform behaviourally to cultural traditions, but have no strong sense of identity with the group.In 'symbolic multiculturalism' members have a sense of identity, but they show no behavioural conformity with the cultural traditions. In the absence of any of the three types of multiculturalism, assimilation to a mainstream culture prevails. It remains an open question which type of multiculturalism is most prevalent in Canada, or whether Canadians are largely assimilationist in the direction of an anglophone or francophone main culture. For purposes of the present paper, only a minimalist definition of multiculturalism is assumed. Canada is multicultural in the sense of being populated by people from diverse ethnic origins.

Since 1971, there have been several studies on attitudes towards the policy as well as to key components therein. The attitudes among the most numerous 'other ethnic' groups[1] towards the policy, and to one of its major components, heritage language preservation, were probed in a survey by O'Bryan, Reitz and Kuplowska (1976). Attitudes toward the policy in general, as well as to heritage language retention specifically, were found to be largely positive. It is interesting to note that this study paid very little, if any, attention to the orientation of ethnic groups towards the larger society. Attitudes towards multiculturalism in the general population were investigated by Berry, Kalin, and Taylor (1977) in a national survey conducted in 1974. Results of that survey, as well as additional investigations have recently been reviewed by Kalin and Berry (1994). Results from a 1991 national survey have been analyzed and reported by

Berry and Kalin (1995). Attitudes towards multiculturalism among majority Canadians can best be described as supportive, but this general support is accompanied by an expectation that ethnic groups should accommodate towards the larger society.

The policy of multiculturalism, as well as research in this area, have focussed primarily on ethnic groups as objects of policy and study (including heritage retention, freedom from discrimination, and sharing with others). The policy and research have been less concerned with the orientation by ethnic groups towards the larger society. This latter topic might be referred to as the citizenship aspects of multiculturalism.[2] Citizenship, in this context, refers to 'membership in a community of shared or common law...' (Pocock, 1992, p.41). Of particular interest are those components of citizenship that consist of allegiance to the 'community as sovereign authority' (Pocock, 1992, p.51). Is citizenship, in the form of allegiance to the country, a given in a multicultural society where retention of particular ethnic heritage is encouraged? While not employing the term 'citizenship', attention to the relations between ethnic groups and the larger society has been given by Berry (1984). He has argued that *integration* is the appropriate mode of acculturation in a multicultural society, where integration refers to the simultaneous desire to maintain cultural heritage and to have positive relations with the larger society.

In plural societies like Canada, a fragmentation of allegiances is a real possibility (Cairns, 1993). One way to reconcile the possible fragmentation is to think of a person's orientation to different groups as being nested. Individuals can feel pride in, and allegiance to, smaller communities (for example, an ethnic group) nested within the larger community of the nation state. Another creative suggestion on how possibly fragmented loyalties can coalesce into a unitary allegiance to a larger community is provided by Breton (1988) in his discussion of two types of nationalism. According to Breton, *ethnic nationalism* (which can also be called cultural or primary) is founded on cultural unity. Here, inclusion or exclusion in a community is based on ethnic factors, such as common ancestry, language, religion and cultural distinctiveness. *Civic nationalism* (also called political, territorial, or secondary), on the other hand, is based on pragmatic and utilitarian factors as forming the basis of the collectivity. In civic nationalism, culture is dissociated from the political. It is Breton's thesis that in anglophone Canada, as well as in francophone Québec, there has been a historical change from ethnic to civic nationalism and that civic nationalism has come to incorporate cultural pluralism.

While direct research on the relations between ethnic groups and the larger society is sparse, the topic of ethnic identity is relevant here and it has enjoyed a substantial amount of research attention in Canada. Ethnic identity has been defined by Driedger (1989) as 'a positive personal attitude and attachment to a group with whom the individual believes he [sic] has a common ancestry based on shared characteristics and shared socio-cultural experiences' (p.162). This definition refers essentially to 'symbolic' ethnicity which Gans (1979) describes as 'love for and a pride in a tradition that can be felt without having to be incorporated in everyday behaviour' (p.9).

Research on ethnic identity is relevant to the question of the relations between ethnic groups and the larger society. In this research respondents are often given the opportunity to select an ethnic as opposed to a national Canadian identity and it becomes possible to assess the relative salience of ethnic group membership and compare it with the salience and importance of being Canadian. Research on ethnic identity in Canada has recently been reviewed by Kalin and Berry (in the press) who concluded that the large majority of Canadians outside Québec identify as 'Canadian'. The most preferred identity in Québec is 'Provincial' (Québécois). Kalin and Berry (in the press) also noted that there has been a decline in the choice of 'Ethnic' identity (including British, French and Other Ethnic) between 1974 and 1991. These authors also concluded that identifying as 'Canadian' does not diminish the acceptance of multiculturalism, and maintaining a heritage identity is compatible with having at the same time a strong Canadian identity and attachment to Canada.

Following the distinction between ethnic and civic nationalism proposed by Breton (1988), it may be useful to speak in terms of ethnic and civic self-identity. Ethnic self-identity refers to self-definition and attachment to a common ancestral group. Civic self-identity, on the other hand, refers to self-definition in terms of, and attachment to, a political entity such as a province or the nation state of Canada.

The purpose of the present study was to examine the citizenship attitudes of Canadians, specifically as they may vary by ethnic origin. Citizenship attitudes were defined in terms of having a Canadian self-identity (as opposed to provincial or ethnic) and having a positive attachment to Canada. Are citizenship attitudes, as discussed here, equally positive among various ethnic groups? Is there a possible cause for concern that ethnic diversity may be associated with widely varying citizenship attitudes?

Method

The present study examined results from a national survey, conducted primarily to investigate attitudes toward multiculturalism and related topics. The assessment of citizenship attitudes in the form of self-identity and Canadianism was an important but limited part of this survey. The survey instrument consisted of 130 questions about attitudes, three concerning identity, and 22 on demography. They were grouped in various ways, separating attitudes, values, beliefs, knowledge, perceptions, evaluations, and self-characterizations. (See Berry and Kalin [1995] for a summary of selected results from this survey.) English and French language versions of the questions were prepared. A copy of the interview schedule is available from Multiculturalism and Citizenship Canada. There were 3325 respondents. This total consisted of a national sample of 2500 adults (over age 18), and over-samples in Montreal, Toronto, and Vancouver to ensure a sample of 500 in each of these three cities. The survey was carried out by Angus Reid in late June and July 1991, using a random telephone dialling procedure. A quota system ensured proportional representation of males and females, as well as the regions of Canada. The analysis by Berry and Kalin (1995) suggests that the sample was reasonably representative of the Canadian population.

To assess self-identity, three questions were asked in the following sequence, near the end of the interview: The first was, 'To which ethnic or cultural group(s) did your ancestors belong?' (If Canadian mentioned, probe: 'Other than Canadian, to which ethnic or cultural group(s) did your ancestors belong?').[3] All responses were recorded, and were tracked as first mention, second mention, and later mention. In a second question, respondents were told, 'People may describe themselves in a number of ways. If you had to choose one, generally speaking, do you think of yourself as:

1. First origin reported (in the first question, for example Dutch),
2. First origin-Canadian (for example Dutch-Canadian),
3. Second origin, if reported (for example Italian),
4. Second origin-Canadian (for example Italian-Canadian),
5. A Province of residence (for example Manitoban),
6. A Canadian,
7. Other (coded as a missing value in subsequent analyses).

All seven choices were read out by the interviewer before respondents gave their choice. From this question the type of identity preferred by a particular respondent was established.

Type of Identity

The following six types of identity were derived.
1. 'Canadian', if respondents selected the Canadian alternative;
2. 'British-Canadian', if they assigned themselves a hyphenated identity in terms of their first or second origin, and that origin was British;
3. 'French-Canadian', if they picked a hyphenated identity in terms of first or second origin, and that origin was French;

4. 'Provincial', if they described themselves in terms of a province;

5. 'Other Ethnic-Canadian', if they selected a hyphenated identity with their first or second origin, and that origin was other than French or British;

6. 'Other National', if they described themselves with their first or second origin without qualifying it with 'Canadian'.

For most of the analyses reported below, 'ethnic' identities were aggregated. That is, after Canadian and Provincial identity, respondents selecting an identity with an 'ethnic' component were treated as one category (that is, British-, French-, or Other Ethnic-Canadian; or Other National).

Strength of Identity

In a third question, respondents were asked, 'Using a 7-point scale where 1 is very weak and 7 is very strong, how strongly do you identify with being …' (the first six options were listed again). This third question was used to assess the strength of each of the identities. For the analyses reported below, strength of ethnic identity consisted of the highest strength rating given to any identity with an ethnic component (that is, British-, French-, or Other Ethnic- Canadian; or Other National).

Canadianism

TABLE 1
CANADIANISM SCALE

1[a]. I am proud to be a Canadian citizen (1n)

2. (…feel about Canada) (Deep attachment=7, Qualified attachment=5, No attachment=3, Join USA=1) (2b)

3. The thought of Québec leaving Canada makes me truly sad (12kk)

4. I am quite willing to listen to others' opinions regarding Canada's future (1o)

5. It is my responsibility as a Canadian citizen to speak out about things that affect the future of this country (1n)

6. I feel less committed to Canada than I did a few years ago (12ll) (R)[b]

7. As a Canadian citizen, I know I have the power to have an effect on Canada's future (1p)

8. More should be done to make Canadians feel proud to be Canadian citizens (3h)

Notes: a. Order of individual items in terms of size of correlation between the item and rest of the scale.
b Item Content is presented in the direction of the survey instrument. For scale construction, items marked R were reversed.

To measure respondents' attachment and commitment to Canada, the Canadianism scale developed by Berry and Kalin (1995) was used. This scale consists of eight opinion statements (see Table 1 for scale). Examples of items are: 'I am proud to be a Canadian citizen', and 'I feel less committed to Canada than I did a few years ago' (responses reversed for this item).

Demographic Variables

Of primary interest was the ethnic origin of respondents. This was ascertained from the question regarding the 'ethnic or cultural group(s) of ancestors' described in detail above. For some analyses, respondents were divided into three groups: British, French and Other Ethnic. For most analyses, the Other Ethnic category was also divided into specific origins categories, if there were at least 30 respondents in the group.Ten groups met this criterion, in addition to British (n=1400) and French (n=745); these were: German (n=242), Italian (n=107), Ukrainian (n=93), Dutch (n=61), Scandinavian (n=61), Chinese (n=48), Polish (n=48), Aboriginal (n=39), Jewish (n= 36), and South Asian (n=33).[4]

An initial examination of the Aboriginal category indicated a disproportionate number of these taking the interview in French. There were 71 respondents who called themselves Aboriginal. Of these, 32 took the interview in French and 20 of these gave their self-identity as Québécois. In the French version of the questionnaire 'Aboriginal person' appeared as 'autochtone'. This term may have been misunderstood by some respondents taking the interview in French. For present analyses, therefore, the Aboriginal category was limited to the 39 respondents who gave the interview in English. Of all the origin categories, 'aboriginal' may be the least representative of aboriginals in the total population. In addition to the possible confusion regarding self-identification in French, the fact that the survey was conducted over the telephone may have meant that aboriginal people may not have had the same equal chance as other Canadians to be included in the sample.

It is not possible to give a precise comparison between the present sample statistics and the results from the 1991 Census. In the present survey, ethnic origin was coded into 'first origin' and 'second origin' mentioned. In the 1991 Census, responses were coded as 'single origins' or 'multiple origins'. When double origins are coded, the problem of 'double counting' occurs, where one person is counted in more than one category. Table 1A of Census Catalogue 93-315 gives single and multiple origin with single counting only. Giving precedence to British over French over Other Ethnic when aggregating multiple origin responses, the following distribution in the Canadian population emerges: British 47.7 per cent, French 24.5 per cent, and Other Ethnic 27.8 per cent. The distribution in the sample was British 43.7 per cent, French 23.2, and Other Ethnic 33.1 per cent.

Results

Type of Identity

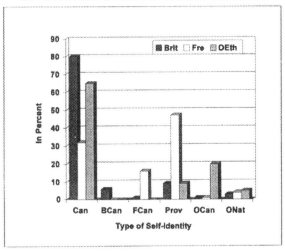

FIGURE 1
SIX TYPES OF SELF-IDENTITY BY THREE ETHNIC ORIGINS

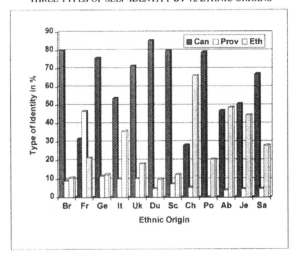

FIGURE 2
THREE TYPES OF SELF-IDENTITY BY 12 ETHNIC ORIGINS

Basic results from the study by Kalin and Berry (in press) regarding the distribution of types of identity in the total sample are given in Figure 1. The predominant identity among Canadians of British origin (80 per cent) and Other Ethnic origin (65 per cent) is Canadian. Among those of French origin, the most frequent choice is Provincial. The various types of ethnic identity are infrequent. When some form of ethnic identity is selected, it is primarily a hyphenated identity. Identity in terms of another nationality is rare. In view of the relatively infrequent selection of ethnic identity, the different types of identity having an ethnic component were aggregated in subsequent analyses.[5]

In order to examine how consistent identity choices are among specific groups in the large category of Other Ethnic, the sample was divided into ten ethnic groups, in addition to British and French. Identity choices in these 12 groups are displayed in Figure 2.[6] Canadian is by far the most frequent identity choice among most of these Other Ethnic groups. Respondents of Chinese origin are an exception, as their most frequent identity is ethnic. The other exception consists of Aboriginal Canadians who selected ethnic identity slightly more frequently than Canadian.

Although there are some differences between respondents of Other Ethnic and British origin, these two categories are far more similar in their choice of identity than either is to French Canadians, who are the most distinct group in terms of identity choice through their frequent selection of Provincial and their relatively less frequent choice of Canadian identity (in

FIGURE 3
CANADIAN IDENTITY BY REGION AND ETHNIC ORIGIN

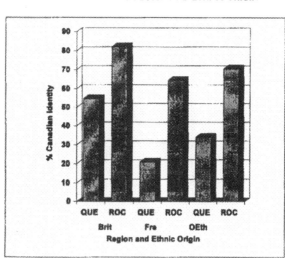

FIGURE 4
PROVINCIAL IDENTITY BY REGION AND ETHNIC ORIGIN

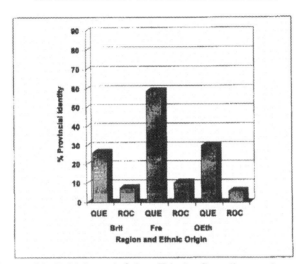

comparison with British and Other Ethnic Canadians). As most French
Canadians reside in Québec, it is important to examine the effects of region
and ethnic origin separately. Figures 3–5 show identity choice as a function
of region and ethnic origin. Figure 3 displays the association of Canadian
identity with both region and ethnic origin. Respondents from Québec from
all ethnic origins are less likely to choose a Canadian identity than
respondents from the rest of Canada. The order of choice of Canadian
identity by ethnic origin is highest among those of British origin, followed
by those of Other Ethnic, and lowest by those of French origin. Provincial
identity is also associated with both region and ethnic origin (see Figure 4).
Respondents from Québec, as compared with those from the rest of Canada,
are more likely to select a Provincial identity. This tendency applies
similarly to respondents from the three ethnic origin categories. Results for
Ethnic identity follow a somewhat different pattern (see Figure 5). Ethnic
identity is more prevalent in the groups which form a minority in a
particular region.

This applies to respondents of British and Other Ethnic origin in Québec
and to those of French origin in the rest of Canada.

Strength of Self-Identity

In addition to selecting a single identity as a self-descriptive term,
respondents were given the option of declaring how strongly they identified
with each of the various types of identity. We should not expect these results
to mirror necessarily those from the categorical choice. It is possible that

respondents may have a relatively strong attachment to other identities, in addition to their preferred one. Also, it may be that respondents reject some of the non-selected identities.

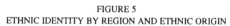

FIGURE 5
ETHNIC IDENTITY BY REGION AND ETHNIC ORIGIN

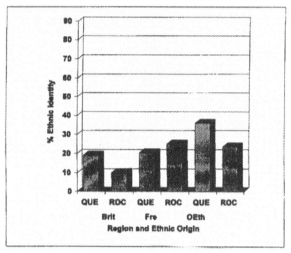

FIGURE 6
STRENGTH OF THREE TYPES OF IDENTITY BY 12 ETHNIC ORIGINS

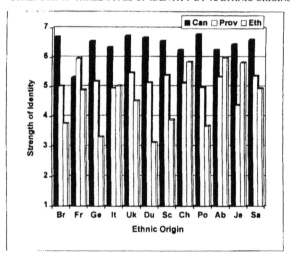

Results on the strength of three identities as a function of ethnic origin are displayed in Figure 6. This Figure shows a number of similarities, but also some differences in comparison with results depicted in Figure 2 (type of identity as a function of ethnic origin). In line with results from the categorical analyses, Canadian identity was rated highest among respondents of British and all of the Other Ethnic origins. It will be recalled that in the categorical analyses, two groups (Chinese and Aboriginal) selected an ethnic identity more frequently than a Canadian (see Figure 2). In the present analyses, even Chinese and Aboriginals rate Canadian identity stronger than ethnic. Among French Canadian respondents, Provincial identity had the highest strength rating. The main difference between the categorical and strength ratings lies in the relative prominence of ethnic as compared with provincial identity. When asked to choose one particular identity, respondents of British and all Other Ethnic origins selected ethnic in second place after Canadian identity. In the strength ratings, the order is reversed for all groups except for Italian, Chinese, Aboriginal, and Jewish, with provincial being more predominant than ethnic.[7]

FIGURE 7
STRENGTH OF CANADIAN IDENTITY BY REGION AND ETHNIC ORIGIN

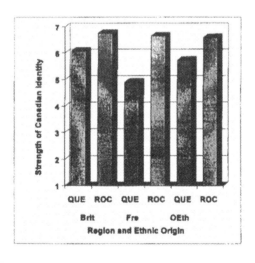

As was the case with the results regarding the choice of one identity, French Canadians are again distinctive in the strength of identity ratings. Their predominant response in both sets of results is provincial identity. To examine the separate influence of ethnic origin and region, results were analyzed as in Figures 7, 8, and 9. Regarding the strength of Canadian identity, region is very important. Respondents from Québec, in each of the three ethnic origin categories, rate Canadian identity less strongly than their counterparts in the rest of Canada. In the rest of Canada, respondents from

FIGURE 8
STRENGTH OF PROVINCIAL IDENTITY BY REGION AND ETHNIC ORIGIN

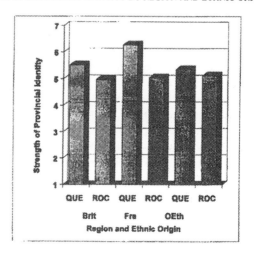

FIGURE 9
STRENGTH OF ETHNIC IDENTITY BY REGION AND ETHNIC ORIGIN

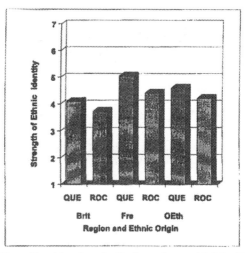

all origins rate Canadian identity similarly and very highly. Ethnic origin is particularly important in Québec, where those of French origin rate Canadian identity less highly than those of British or Other Ethnic origin. The pattern of results for provincial identity is similar, except in the opposite direction. Québec residents rate provincial identity more highly than those from outside Québec. Outside Québec, the rating of provincial identity is virtually the same among all groups. The distinctive group, in having particularly high ratings for provincial identity, consists of French Canadians in Québec. Results on the strength of ethnic identity are displayed in Figure 9. Living in Québec, as compared with living in the rest of Canada, has an influence on how highly respondents rate ethnic identity, with Québec residents assigning higher ratings to ethnic identity than those living outside. An interesting difference between the strength ratings and the categorical choices presented in Figure 5 is in the column depicting French Canadians in Québec. In the identity choice results, relatively fewer French Canadians living in Québec, as compared with those living outside, selected an ethnic identity. However, French Canadians in Québec rated ethnic identity more highly than French Canadians outside.

FIGURE 10
CANADIANISM BY 12 ETHNIC ORIGINS

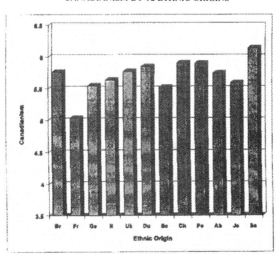

Results pertaining to Canadianism, defined as attachment to Canada, are presented in Figure 10. Canadians of French origin show a lower level of Canadianism than the other two groups.[x] A more detailed analysis, involving the 12 origin groups, is presented in Figure 11. Statistical tests reveal that respondents of French origin have significantly lower levels of Canadianism than respondents of all groups, except for those from Aboriginal, Jewish, and Scandinavian origin.[9] The other groups are not significantly different from each other. Analyses by region and ethnic origin together are shown in Figure 11. The pattern of results in Figure 11 is very similar to that in Figures 3 and 7. Québec respondents from all three origin groups show a lower level of Canadianism than respondents from the three groups residing in the rest of Canada. What is again particularly noteworthy in Figure 11 is the distinctive position of French Canadians residing in Québec.[10]

FIGURE 11
CANADIANISM BY REGION AND ETHNIC ORIGIN

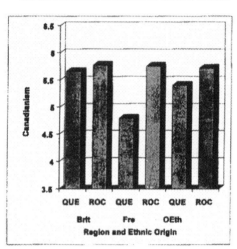

Discussion

Citizenship attitudes can be characterized as being very positive in Canada outside Québec. Canadian identity (in comparison with provincial or ethnic identity) is the predominant choice and is most strongly rated among those of British and Other Ethnic origin. These groups also score very high on Canadianism, a scale measuring attachment to Canada. Being citizens of Canada appears to be more important to a sizeable majority of British and Other Ethnic origin than being members of particular ethnic groups. In this sense, Canadians in the rest of Canada are assimilationist regarding themselves, even though they are relatively tolerant towards ethnically diverse others (Kalin and Berry, 1994). This assimilation is not an ethnic assimilation, in the sense of anglo-conformity (Palmer, 1976) that characterized an earlier period in Canadian history. The assimilation is civic and presumably based on an attachment to the nation state of Canada.

To be sure, the relative predominance of Canadian vs. ethnic identity is not uniform among all Other Ethnic groups. The greatest ethnic affirmation exists among Chinese, Aboriginals and Jews. Sizeable proportions of these groups prefer an ethnic identity. However, the preference for an ethnic identity does not appear to imply a rejection of Canada. On the contrary, respondents of Chinese, Aboriginal and Jewish background rated the strength of their Canadian identity as being very high and also scored high on Canadianism. The term *integration* (Berry, 1984), referring to the simultaneous desire to maintain ethnic heritage and positive relations to the larger society, is an appropriate description of this pattern of results. It appears, therefore, that an ethnic self-identity can be nested within a strong Canadian civic identity. In this sense, ethnic heritage identity is quite compatible with a strong national civic identity.

The most notable result of the present investigation is the distinct profile of citizenship attitudes found among residents from Québec who had the lowest preference for a Canadian identity. They also rated the strength of Canadian identity the lowest and scored the lowest on Canadianism. Their preferred identity was provincial (Québécois) which they also rated as very strong. In addition to having to reconcile ethnic with civic identity, residents of Québec must orient themselves towards two nations, namely Canada and Québec. Québec nationalism is clearly evident in the results of the present investigation. What is less clear, however, is the degree of compatibility versus conflict between Canadian and Québec nationalism. On the one hand, we have the finding that Québec residents rate provincial identity the strongest. On the other hand, results showed that Quebeckers rate Canadian identity positively (nearly 5 out of a possible 7 for Quebeckers of French origin, approximately 6 for Quebeckers of British origin and nearly 6 for those of Other Ethnic origin), and also score relatively highly on Canadianism (Quebeckers of French origin scoring nearly 5 out of a possible 7, and those of British and Other Ethnic origin scoring over 5) leading to the suggestion that Québec nationalism *within* Canada is a strong attitudinal option. An interesting question concerns the relative importance of ethnic as opposed to civic factors in the attitudinal patterns reflecting Québec nationalism. While a conclusive answer to this question is not possible from the present results, there are suggestions that civic factors play an important role. It will be recalled that Québec nationalist attitudes were not limited to Québec residents of French origin, but were also manifest to some extent among Quebeckers of British and Other Ethnic origin. Such results are entirely compatible with the analysis by Breton (1988) that Québec nationalism is becoming increasingly civic and may well include cultural pluralism. A strong case that Québec is becoming increasingly multicultural has also been made by Balthazar (1994).

The assumption was made in the present article that citizenship attitudes are reflected in the choice of type of identity, in the strength ratings of several identities, and by the scale measuring attachment to Canada. To what extent do these different measures of citizenship attitudes provide a consistent picture? Consistency in measures was demonstrated in the highly positive citizenship attitudes among Canadians of British and Other Ethnic origins. The pattern of results in this regard was highly similar regarding the preference for and ratings of strength of Canadian identity as well as high scores on Canadianism. Similarly, there was consistency in the lower preference for, and lower strength ratings of Canadian identity among residents from Québec in general and from French origin in particular. Consistency was also shown across measures in the higher preference for provincial identity among Québec residents, in particular those of French origin. These consistent results provide validity to the measures used, suggesting that they are indicative of a common underlying dimension, namely citizenship attitudes.

The major discrepancy among the measures pertains to the inversion of the order of preference for an ethnic identity versus a provincial identity. On the basis of the measure of choice of a particular type of identity, the emerging order of predominance for those of British and Other Ethnic origin is first Canadian, then ethnic, and then provincial. The results from the strength ratings of those with several types of identity suggest a different order, namely, Canadian, then provincial, then ethnic. The apparent discrepancy can be reconciled by remembering that relatively small minorities selected the ethnic identity (11 per cent of those of British origin, and 25 per cent of those of Other Ethnic origin). All respondents, whether they selected a given identity or not, had the opportunity to rate the strength of all identities. The large majorities who did not select an ethnic identity may have given ethnic identity a sufficiently low strength rating to result in its relegation to the end of the order. It is possible, therefore, that ethnic identity is an identity from which some Canadians distance themselves. This self-distancing from ethnicity suggests that Canada may be less truly multicultural than official rhetoric might imply.

Conclusions

In Canada outside Québec, citizenship attitudes, in the sense of having a Canadian identity and a feeling of attachment to Canada, are remarkably positive. Civic national identity and attachment to the nation state of Canada are far more important to a large majority of Canadians than attachment to a particular heritage group.There are relatively few differences in these attitudes among various 'Other Ethnic' groups. There is some ethnic affirmation, among the Other Ethnic groups, but this is accompanied by a concurrent strong attachment to Canada. There are also suggestions that many Canadians distance themselves from ethnicity and embrace instead a civic nationalism.

In Québec, a distinctive pattern of citizenship attitudes prevails reflecting Québec nationalism. Primary affiliation among a majority of residents is provincial, and Canadian identity and Canadianism is less strong than in the rest of Canada. This pattern of attitudes applies not only to those of French origin, but also, to some extent, to those with British and Other Ethnic roots, which suggests that Québec nationalism is more a civic than simply an ethnic phenomenon. However, Canadianism and Canadian identity are still sufficiently strong in Québec that the idea of the nation of Québec within the nation state of Canada is an attitudinal possibility.

NOTES

This article reports analyses of a national survey conducted in June 1991 by Angus Reid and commissioned by Multiculturalism and Citizenship Canada. The survey included questions developed by J. W. Berry and the present author. The interpretations expressed in this article are those of the author and do not necessarily reflect the views of Multiculturalism and Citizenship Canada. A version of this article was presented at a symposium on 'Ethnicity and Citizenship', held on 5 February 1994 at the Institute of Interethnic Relations, University of Ottawa. The symposium was sponsored by the Academy of the Humanities and Social Sciences of the Royal Society of Canada.

1. The term 'other ethnic' is used in this paper to refer to groups whose origin is other than British or French.
2. This gap in the policy may have been a concern to the former Conservative Government when it added 'Citizenship' to Multiculturalism when it became a separate Federal Department. Under the Liberal Government, elected in 1993, multiculturalism and citizenship were again assigned to different Federal Departments.
3. This question is very similar to the one asked in the 1986 Census. There, the question was 'To which ethnic or cultural group(s) do you or did your ancestors belong?'. In the 1991 Census, the question was 'To which ethnic or cultural group(s) did this person's ancestors belong?'.
4. The 'British' group is an aggregation of English, Irish, Scottish, and Welsh. 'French' includes Québécois, Franco-Ontarian, Franco-Manitoban, Acadian. 'Scandinavian' is the aggregation of Danish, Scandinavian, Swedish, Norwegian, and Icelandic. 'South Asian' applies to Hindu, Indian, Sikh, Punjabi and Tamil.
5. In addition to the graphic presentation of the results, tests of statistical significance were applied. In the case of frequency data, ChiSquare analyses were calculated. To analyze mean differences, regression based analyses of variance were employed. The SAS System 6.03 was used for all analyses. The ChiSquare analyses of the contingency table forming the basis of Figure 3 was 700.23, $p < .001$.
6. ChiSquare for results in Figure 4 = 798.68, $p < .001$.
7. Analyses of variance conducted on the strength ratings revealed highly significant F ratios for ethnicity for each of the three identities. For Canadian identity $F(2) = 266.45$, $p < .001$ (with all origin comparisons being significant at alpha = .01), for provincial identity $F = 54.94$, $p < .001$ (with French origin respondents being significantly higher than the other two groups), and for ethnic identity $F = 60.28$, $p < .001$ (with all group comparisons being significant).
8. Analysis of variance yielded an $F(2)$ for ethnic origin of 139.24, $p < .001$. French Canadian respondents are significantly lower than the other two groups, who are not different from each other at alpha = .01, according to a Scheffe test.
9. F (11) for ethnic origin = 26.77, $p < .001$. with the exception of the lower scores of respondents of French origin, none of the other groups are significantly different from each other.
10. Analysis of variance results are as follows. For ethnic origin, $F = 25.24$, $p < .001$, for region $F = 79.82$, $p < .001$, for interaction between ethnic origin and region, $F = 25.20$, $p < .001$.

REFERENCES

Angus Reid Group (1991) *Multiculturalism and Canadians: Attitude Study 1991*, report submitted to Multiculturalism and Citizenship Canada.

Balthazar, L. (1994) *Un Québec francophone et multiethnique: Une citoyenneté particulière*, paper presented at the symposium 'Ethnicity and Citizenship', Institute of Interethnic Relations, University of Ottawa, 5 February 1994.

Berry, J.W. (1984) 'Multicultural Policy in Canada: A Social Psychological Analysis', *Canadian Journal of Behavioural Science*, Vol.16, pp.353–370.

Berry, J.W., Kalin, R. and Taylor, D. (1977) *Multiculturalism and Ethnic Attitudes in Canada*, Ottawa: Supply and Services Canada.

Berry, J.W. and Kalin, R. (1995) *Multicultural and Ethnic Attitudes in Canada: An Overview of the 1991 National Survey*, Canadian Journal of Behavioural Science, Vol.27, No.3, pp.301–20.

Breton, R. (1964) 'Institutional Completeness of Ethnic Communities and Personal Relations to Immigrants', *American Journal of Sociology*, Vol.70, pp.193–205.

Breton, R. (1988) 'From Ethnic to Civic Nationalism: English Canada and Québec', *Ethnic and Racial Studies*, Vol.11, No.1, pp.85–102.

Burnet, J. (1976) 'Ethnicity: Canadian Experience and Policy', *Sociological Focus*, Vol.9, pp.199–207.

Burnet, J. (1978) 'The Policy of Multiculturalism within a Bilingual Framework', *Canadian Ethnic Studies*, Vol.10, No.2, pp.107–113.

Burnet, J. (1984) 'Myths and Multiculturalism', in R. J. Samuda, J. W. Berry, and M. Laferriere (eds) , *Multiculturalism in Canada*, Toronto: Allyn and Bacon, Inc.

Cairns, A. C. (1993) 'The Fragmentation of Canadian Citizenship', in W. Kaplan (ed) *Belonging: The Meaning and Future of Canadian Citizenship*, Montreal and Kingston: McGill-Queen's University Press.

Driedger, L. (1989) *The Ethnic Factor: Identity in Diversity*, Toronto: McGraw Hill Ryerson.

Gans, H.J. (1979) 'Symbolic Ethnicity: The future of Ethnic Groups and Culture in America', *Ethnic and Racial Studies*, Vol.2, pp.1–20.

Isajiw, W. W. (1980) 'Definitions of Ethnicity', in J. E. Goldstein and R. M. Bienvenue (eds), *Ethnicity and Ethnic Relations in Canada*, Toronto: Butterworths.

Kalin, R. and Berry, J.W. (1994) 'Ethnic and Multicultural Attitudes' in J. W. Berry and J. Laponce (eds) *Ethnicity and Culture in Canada: The research landscape*, Toronto: University of Toronto Press.

Kalin, R. and Berry, J. W. (in press), 'Ethnic, National and Provincial Self-Identity in Canada: Analyses of 1974 and 1991 National Surveys', *Canadian Ethnic Studies*.

Li, P.S. (1990) 'Race and Ethnicity', in P.S. Li (ed) *Race and Ethnic Relations in Canada*, Toronto: Oxford University Press.

O'Bryan, K., Reitz, J. and Kuplowska, O. (1976) *Nonofficial Languages: A Study in Canadian Multiculturalism*, Ottawa: Supply and Services Canada.

Palmer, H. (1976) *Reluctant hosts: Report of the Second Canadian Conference on Multiculturalism*, Ottawa: Canadian Consultative Council on Multiculturalism, pp.81–118.

Pocock, J. G. A. (1992) 'The Ideal of Citizenship since Classical Times', *Queen's Quarterly*, Vol.99, No.1, pp.33–55.

Porter, J. (1980) 'Canada: Dilemmas and Contradictions of a Multi-Ethnic Society', In J. E. Goldstein and R. M. Bienvenue (eds) *Ethnicity and Ethnic Relations in Canada*, Toronto: Butterworths.

Roberts, L.W. and Clifton, R.A. (1990) 'Multiculturalism in Canada: A Social Perspective', in Peter S. Li (ed), *Race and ethnic relations in Canada*, Toronto: Oxford Univ Press

Russell, P.H. (1994) *Ethnicity, Citizenship and the Constitution*, Paper presented at the symposium 'Ethnicity and Citizenship', Institute of Interethnic Relations, University of Ottawa, 5 February 1994.

Feelings of Fraternity towards Old and New Canadians: the Interplay of Ethnic and Civic Factors

LESLIE S. LACZKO

How are feelings of fraternity distributed within nation-states? Most theories of
citizenship take for granted that citizens of modern societies will extend higher levels
of fraternity towards fellow citizens than towards 'foreigners' who are citizens of other
states. At the same time, past research on the status dimension of ethnic stratification
in Canada shows that status evaluations are highest for the British and European
groups, and lowest for non-white groups. This article formulates a series of hypotheses
on the way ethnic and civic factors combine in shaping feelings of fraternity in
Canada. The hypotheses are empirically assessed through a secondary analysis of data
from a 1991 survey of the Canadian population. The results show that Canadian civic
experience is universally valued throughout the Canadian population, even as ethnic
characteristics of fellow citizens continue to be differentially evaluated.

Introduction

To what extent are feelings of fraternity shaped by 'national' boundaries in
the contemporary international system? How important is local civic
experience as a determinant of how feelings of fraternity are allocated? And
how are feelings of fraternity structured within the boundaries of a
particular state? These are the questions that this article will explore with a
look at some recent data on one particular 'national' society,[1] Canada.

One of the lasting intellectual and ideological legacies of the French
Revolution was the idea that there is a complex link between liberty,
equality, and fraternity. In the ideology of the modern nation-state that took
root in France and has been widely diffused, a modern society is a national
community of free and equal individuals, whose fraternal feelings of
solidarity flow from the shared experience of equal participation in public
life. More generally, the (ideal-typical) national society has been viewed,
for much of the past century, as the principal and in many cases exclusive
setting in which feelings of solidarity get focused and organized.[2] In this
view, which has influenced most theories of citizenship, it is only natural (as
well as fitting and proper) that citizens of a given state should feel more

solidarity with fellow 'nationals' than with 'foreigners' who are citizens of other states. This general postulate has been central to much theoretical thinking about modern societies and states since the French Revolution.

In recent years, this received view of the 'naturalness' and centrality of the nation-state has been increasingly questioned and challenged.[3] With respect to theories of citizenship, the editors of a recent collection of essays note that a central problematic weakness of the traditional perspectives is their

> ...location of citizenship within the geographical and cultural boundaries of the nation-state. This once-unquestioned terrain of membership has today disintegrated–as a consequence of the internal fragmentation in the structure of multi-ethnic societies, on the one hand, and of the development towards supranational economic and political institutions, on the other.[4]

Just who is a fellow citizen, and who is eligible to become one? Citizenship norms in the contemporary international system display considerable variation. In many states, for example Germany, real or putative ethnic origins have historically provided the central criterion for defining eligibility for full membership in the political community. A few other states, notably France, have historically developed an ideology of citizenship that downplayed the ethnic factor and emphasized and celebrated the primacy of shared French experience. This conception of the modern nation posited that citizenship was based on shared experience, rather than on origins or ethnicity or race or religion. This type of contrast[5] illustrates the ideal-typical distinction between ethnic and civic nationalism.[6] Many modern states, however, have evolved citizenship norms that involve some combination of ethnic and civic factors. This has certainly been true of Canada.[7] The evolving national identity of Canada has always been fragmented, as a result of various factors: the country's origins as a new world society which incorporated aboriginal populations, its federal structure, its historical French-English dualism and its experience of continuous settlement and immigration. At the same time, Canada's history as a British dominion and its geographical position as a neighbour of the United States have produced a society that has always been permeable to outside influences. In this context, Canada provides an interesting arena in which to examine the way ethnic and civic factors intermesh and combine.

This article explores the interplay of ethnic and civic factors in shaping the structure of feelings of fraternity in Canada. Does fraternal solidarity flow from the knowledge of shared Canadian experience, or from the operation of an entrenched ethnic pecking order? Does the impact of shared Canadian experience override, simply coexist with, or exacerbate the impact of ethnic factors on feelings of fraternity? How do respondents combine ethnic and civic cues to determine feelings of fraternity? Does perceived citizenship status make a difference? Do respondents react more favourably towards fellow citizens of a given ethnic origin who were born and raised in Canada than towards recently-arrived immigrants (of the same ethnic origin)? How does the magnitude of this civic experience effect compare with the magnitude of the differences produced by the series of specific ethnic and national labels? That is, do fellow citizens elicit higher fraternity ratings than new immigrants regardless of their ethnic origin, or are some new immigrants allocated higher levels of fraternity than some fellow citizens?

Previous Research

The research carried out over the years on the status dimension of ethnic stratification, as well as the work dealing with social distance towards ethnic groups is relevant here, even if most of it did not deal explicitly with feelings of fraternity. For example, the studies of Berry, Kalin and Taylor[8] as well as Pineo[9] revealed that the Canadian population, in the 1960s and 1970s, systematically gave the highest status evaluations to those of British origin, with evaluations following a downward gradient through various European origins, with the lowest evaluations being reserved for non-whites. Bibby's national surveys[10] found a slight increase in the proportion of the population feeling 'at ease' with visible minorities between 1975 and 1985. At the same time, it has been widely assumed that Canadians react more favorably to someone who is 'born and raised in Canada' than to someone born elsewhere, although there has been very little systematic research on this issue, either in the Canadian context or elsewhere. One recent study of the determinants of prestige in two Western Canadian cities found that nativity (being born in Canada) has a small positive effect on prestige evaluations, but that nativity is much less important than occupation and ethnicity in shaping prestige evaluations.[11]

This article is not about social standing per se, or what the stratification literature refers to as deference entitlements.[12] Rather, the article is about feelings of fraternity. The two concepts are distinct theoretically, and it is unclear whether judgments of high social standing necessarily coincide with feelings of fraternity when studied empirically. This article investigates specifically how perceptions of ethnic status and civic status combine to shape feelings of fraternity.

Methods and Procedure

These questions are addressed with standard statistical techniques using data from the 1991 Angus Reid/Multiculturalism and Citizenship attitude survey (N=3325, see Appendix for details). This data set contains two sets of measures that are analyzed here. In the first set of 13 measures (series A), respondents are asked:

> I would like you to think of recent immigrants to Canada. These are people who were born and raised outside of Canada. How comfortable would you feel being around individuals from the following groups of immigrants. How about...(read British first outside of Quebec, French first in Quebec, then rotate)

For each of 13 ethno-national group labels, respondents are asked to rate 'how comfortable' they would feel with recent immigrant members of the group on a 7 point scale, with 1 = not at all comfortable and 7= completely comfortable.

In the second set of 14 measures (series B), respondents are asked:

> Now I would like you to think of people born and raised in Canada, who have different ethnic and cultural origins. How comfortable would you feel being around individuals from the following groups. How about persons having...(read British first outside Quebec, French first in Quebec, then rotate)

Here again, respondents rate their comfort level on a 7 point scale. The second series of measures, referring to the origins of people born and raised in Canada, uses exactly the same labels as the first series referring to recent immigrants. (In addition the second series includes a measure dealing with Native Canadian Indians.)

A comparison of these 13 pairs of scores allows a clear assessment of the impact of civic experience on feelings of social distance or fraternity. For each pair, the difference in scores gives a measure of the importance of perceived Canadian nativity and life experience in allocating feelings of fraternity. The comparison that respondents are making (or rather that we shall infer they are making, based on the statistical results) is between those fellow Canadians whose cumulative Canadian experience is 100 per cent of their lifetime, and those who, although born and raised outside of Canada, have been admitted to citizenship candidacy status by the Canadian state, but whose cumulative Canadian life experience is still close to zero. Note that this contrast is not the same as the familiar demographic nativity indicator (born in Canada/outside Canada) often used in the social sciences in Canada. In the latter contrast, the group of respondents born outside Canada is very heterogeneous in that it includes people who have many decades of Canadian life experience as well as people who have only recently arrived.

Theoretical Questions and Hypotheses

In this study design the respondents provide a rating of their feelings of fraternity based on two cues: an ethno-national label, and an indication of citizenship status. How do respondents 'process' these simultaneously-received cues? Several hypotheses can be advanced to as to the way ethnic and civic factors combine in shaping feelings of fraternity.

The Sign or Direction of the Civic Experience Effect

Are respondents more comfortable with those who have Canadian experience, or is foreign experience more valued? Three mutually exclusive hypotheses can be formulated as to the direction of the relationship between citizenship status (new immigrant or born Canadian) and feelings of fraternity.

Hypothesis 1A: The civic experience effect will be positive. Across all ethno-national labels, fraternity ratings will be higher for those born and raised in Canada than for those who have just arrived. This follows from the literature on citizenship as based on shared and accumulated Canadian experience. In this perspective, someone whose Canadian experience credentials include nativity and childhood will elicit a higher fraternity rating than someone who has as yet accumulated very little in the way of direct Canadian life experience.

Hypothesis 1B: The civic experience effect will be modest or near zero. Put differently, the impact of citizenship status will be negligible: there will be no significant difference between the fraternity ratings allocated to new immigrants and to born Canadians. In the modern world system, this would be likely in societies with a short history, a very weak national civic culture, and in which the influence of trans-national ethno-national categories is relatively strong. It would also be likely in some ideal-typical world system where 'national' boundaries are completely unimportant, and individuals are 'citizens of the world'.

Hypothesis 1C: The civic experience effect will be negative. In other words, the fraternity scores elicited by new immigrants will be higher than those elicited by those born and raised in Canada. This possibility would be likely in societies with a long colonial history, and/or with a low level of civic trust, for example in long-lasting totalitarian regimes. In such extreme contexts, one might expect people to be more comfortable with newly arrived immigrants than with established natives.

FIGURE 1

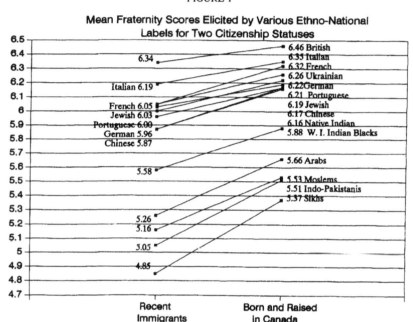

Mean Fraternity Scores Elicited by Various Ethno-National Labels for Two Citizenship Statuses

Assessment: As Figure 1 shows, the civic experience effect is indeed positive for all ethno-national labels, as predicted by hypothesis 1. The fraternity scores for the second series of measures on the right are all systematically higher than the scores for the first series of measures on the left. For each ethno-national label, respondents are more comfortable with someone if that person was born and raised in Canada.

The Magnitude of the Civic Experience Effect across All Labels

Is the civic effect (or preference for Canadian experience) of equal magnitude across the set of all ethno-national labels, or is it more important for some labels than for others? Two hypotheses can be put forward:

Hypothesis 2A: The magnitude of the civic experience effect will be the same across the list of ethno-national labels. In other words, information about citizenship status combines independently and *additively* with information about ethno-national labels in influencing fraternity scores. This would occur if Canadian experience credentials operate along the lines of a civil society analogue of a universal benefit, increasing fraternity scores equally whatever the ethnic origin.

Hypothesis 2B: The magnitude of the civic experience effect will not be the same for all ethno-national labels. In this view, the cue for Canadian experience will be more important in increasing feelings of fraternity for some labels than for others. In other words, ethnic and civic factors will combine *interactively.* This would occur if Canadian credentials operate on a sliding scale or along the lines of a means-tested or defined target group benefit, having more of an impact on fraternity scores for some ethnic labels than for others.

Assessment: If we turn to Figure 1 once again, we can see that the results, when looked at from a distance, tend to support hypothesis 2A, since the slopes are all positive. A closer look, however, reveals that there is also support for hypothesis 2B, since the magnitude of the civic experience effect is not quite the same for all ethno-national labels. Its importance increases as one goes down the scale from British to Sikh labels. Canadian experience increases the mean level of fraternity extended to the British label by 0.12, to the Ukrainian label by 0.21, to the West Indian Black label by 0.30, to the Arab label by 0.40, and to the Sikh label by 0.52. One process at work could be that Canadian experience credentials are more important in allocating fraternity towards those groups about which less is known or with which a respondent is less familiar. In general, the higher the fraternity score elicited by an ethno-national label, the lower the distinct positive effect of Canadian experience. It is the British label for which the civic experience effect has the lowest slope, suggesting that for this label the extra positive effect of Canadian experience is lower than for all other labels. (This point will be returned to in the discussion.)

Does shared Canadian experience increase consensus?

Independently of its impact on the overall *level* of feelings of fraternity, we can hypothesize that shared Canadian experience should have a positive impact on the level of *consensus* surrounding the allocation of feelings of fraternity. This follows from the view that Canadian experience will have the effect of reducing the level of dispersion surrounding levels of fraternity. This can be tested in three different ways:

Hypothesis 3A: The range from maximum to minimum across ethno-national labels will be lower for the series of measures dealing with those born and raised in Canada than for the series of measures dealing with recently arrived immigrants.

Assessment: Again from Figure 1, we can see that this hypothesis is confirmed. The range from British to Sikh is 1.49 in the first series on the left, and 1.09 in the second series on the right.

Hypothesis 3B: In each of the 13 pairs of ethno-national comparisons, the effect of Canadian experience will be to reduce the standard deviation of the scores. This would reflect the greater consensus surrounding fraternity ratings for those with Canadian experience credentials.

Assessment: Figure 2 gives the standard deviations of all 26 measures. This hypothesis is clearly confirmed as well. For each ethno-national label,

FIGURE 2

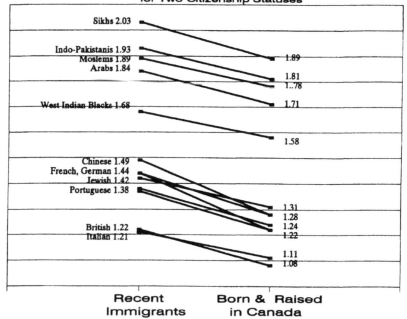

Consensus Levels* Elicited by Various Ethno-National Labels for Two Citizenship Statuses

Sikhs 2.03

Indo-Pakistanis 1.93
Moslems 1.89
Arabs 1.84

1.89
1.81
1..78

West Indian Blacks 1.68

1.71

1.58

Chinese 1.49
French, German 1.44
Jewish 1.42
Portuguese 1.38

1.31
1.28
British 1.22
Italian 1.21

1.24
1.22

1.11
1.08

Recent Immigrants   Born & Raised in Canada

* Entries are standard deviations. The lower the standard deviation, the higher the consensus level.

Canadian experience increases the consensus level. It is also clear that the higher mean scores also have the higher consensus levels. Also, in this case the magnitude of the civic experience effect in increasing consensus *is* roughly the same across all ethno-national labels.

Hypothesis 3C: The strong and powerful effect of shared Canadian experience will scramble and mix-up the ethno-national pecking order. In other words, in this view the rank order of fraternity ratings for the second series of measures should be substantially different from the rank order of the first series. The logic here is that the civic norms of valuing shared Canadian experience will, if they are strong enough, override the influence of the ethno-national hierarchy.

Assessment: From Figure 1 again, it is clear that this hypothesis is not confirmed. The rank order from high to low of the first series dealing with new immigrants correlates almost perfectly with the rank order of the second series dealing with Canadians born and raised. So, on the whole, shared civic experience raises the mean levels of fraternity, decreases the range from maximum to minimum across the set of all labels, and increases the level of consensus around each mean level, but does not seriously scramble or alter the ethnic pecking order.

Hypothesis 4: Knowing that someone has Canadian experience should reduce uncertainty about how much fraternity should be extended to that person. Accordingly, one would expect the second series of measures, dealing with people born and raised in Canada, to display fewer indeterminate answers ('don't know' and 'no answer') than the first series.

Assessment: In the first series 8.4 percent of the respondents gave one or more indeterminate answers as opposed to 7.4 percent for the second series. This difference, although slight, is in the predicted direction and lends support to the hypothesis.

Is the civic experience effect found among immigrants ?

Hypothesis 5: Another indication of the active operation of shared Canadian civic norms would be revealed if the civic effect, or preference for Canadian experience, was to be found even among those respondents who are themselves born outside Canada.

Assessment: This hypothesis is confirmed, as Table 1 indicates. The civic experience effect is just as strong among respondents born outside Canada as among those who are Canadian-born. In other words, the preference for Canadian experience is broadly distributed across the population and in no way concentrated among those who were themselves born in Canada.

TABLE I
AVERAGE FRATERNITY SCORES FOR TWO SETS OF MEASURES, BY
RESPONDENT'S OWN BIRTHPLACE

		SERIES A	SERIES B
RESPONDENT	YES	5.71	6.01
BORN IN		(2776)	(2772)
CANADA?	NO	5.77	6.09
		(543)	(542)

SERIES A: MEAN SCORE OF MEASURES REFERRING TO NEWLY-ARRIVED IMMIGRANTS

SERIES B: MEAN SCORE OF MEASURES REFERRING TO PEOPLE BORN AND RAISED IN
CANADA

The Structure of Feelings of Fraternity

How are the measures related to each other? Three hypotheses can be put
forth:

Hypothesis 6A: There will be positive correlations between each of the
measures in the first set (13 x 13=169), and the same for the measures in the
second set. In this view, feeling comfortable with members of any given
ethno-national label will be associated with feelings of comfort with
members of any other ethno-national label. This follows from the
assumption that whatever their differences, the groups are sufficiently
similar that feelings of fraternity are to some extent transferable from one
target group to the other.

Hypothesis 6B: The correlations within each set will be close to zero, and
exhibit no systematic structure.This follows from the work of Converse
which suggests that many attitudes in mass publics are just simply not all
that structured.[13] In this case, this possibility would occur if each of the
ethno-national labels elicits meanings that are completely different from any
of the others. This would presumably be possible in a very highly
segmented society, where knowledge of any one label would be only
weakly related to knowledge about any other label.

Hypothesis 6C: There will be negative correlations between all or some of
the measures within each of the two sets. This would be true if the
distribution of feelings of fraternity were a zero-sum affair, with positive
feelings towards some group(s) being negatively associated with feelings
towards some other group(s). In this perspective it might be expected that,

for example, negative or lukewarm feelings towards Sikhs would be associated with positive feelings towards the British or French or some other label. The logic of this argument is that there might be a compensation mechanism at work. Extending a low level of fraternity towards one group would be a way of conserving it and then redistributing it towards another group.

Assessment: Hypothesis 6A is clearly supported. As Table 2 shows, all correlations in each set are strongly positive, with the vast majority of coefficients above 0.4.

Hypothesis 7A: Following the logic of earlier hypotheses, it could be expected that shared Canadian experience induces a tighter structure, or greater connectedness, in the second series, dealing with those who have Canadian experience credentials. Accordingly, for each pair of measures, their correlation in the second series should be somewhat higher than their correlation in the first series, dealing with new immigrants.

Hypothesis 7B: If on the other hand, the national context is one in which new immigrants are seen as 'foreigners', and if foreigners are perceived as an undifferentiated category whose members are similar to each other simply by virtue of their being foreigners, it could be expected that feelings towards new immigrants will be more highly structured than feelings towards fellow citizens. In this view, shared civic experience functions in a way that allows people to get to know each other and thereby breaks down the stereotype of foreigners as a unified category. Accordingly, it would be expected that for each pair of measures, their correlation in the second series should be somewhat lower than their correlation in the first series.

Assessment: Hypothesis 7A is clearly supported. For each pair of measures, the correlations in series B are slightly higher than their counterparts in series A. This suggests that shared Canadian experience has the effect of slightly 'tightening' the structure of feelings of fraternity. A significant exception is found in the correlations involving the French ethnic label. For these pairs there is no systematic difference between the correlations dealing with immigrants and those dealing with Canadians born and raised. Furthermore, these correlations are lower than the others, suggesting that the French label evokes a distinct pattern of responses, a point to which we shall return shortly.

Hypothesis 8: Along the lines developed earlier, another sign of a civic experience effect would be revealed by carrying out a principal components factor analysis of each set of measures, and then comparing the two sets of results. If shared Canadian experience exerts an extremely powerful effect

TABLE 2
CORRELATIONS AND FACTOR ANALYSES OF FRATERNITY SCORES FOR TWO SETS OF MEASURES

A. MEASURES REFERRING TO RECENT IMMIGRANTS

	B	F	U	S	I	G	C	W	J	A	I	P	Factor 1	Factor 2
British	1.00												.65	.47
French	.42	1.00											.63	.19
Ukrainians	.60	.49	1.00										.79	.27
Sikhs	.37	.42	.54	1.00									.79	-.46
Indo-Pakistanis	.39	.44	.55	.87	1.00								.82	-.42
Germans	.59	.47	.67	.49	.52	1.00							.76	.29
Chinese	.47	.45	.63	.60	.63	.63	1.00						.81	.02
West Indian Blacks	.40	.42	.52	.65	.70	.53	.68	1.00					.79	-.21
Jews	.60	.45	.65	.50	.53	.59	.61	.61	1.00				.78	.25
Arabs	.41	.46	.57	.74	.76	.56	.61	.63	.59	1.00			.84	-.31
Italians	.54	.53	.63	.48	.52	.61	.63	.58	.65	.59	1.00		.80	.27
Portuguese	.53	.51	.66	.56	.60	.63	.67	.62	.66	.64	.80	1.00	.84	.16
Moslems	.42	.47	.57	.78	.79	.52	.62	.56	.58	.84	.58	.65	.84	-.35

B. MEASURES REFERRING TO PEOPLE BORN AND RAISED IN CANADA

	B	F	U	S	I	G	C	W	J	A	I	P	Factor 1	Factor 2
British	1.00												.68	.48
French	.43	1.00											.60	.19
Ukrainians	.67	.47	1.00										.80	.29
Sikhs	.42	.43	.57	1.00									.82	-.42
Indo-Pakistanis	.44	.44	.58	.89	1.00								.85	-.39
Germans	.64	.47	.70	.52	.54	1.00							.77	.33
Chinese	.51	.44	.63	.61	.65	.65	1.00						.82	.06
West Indian Blacks	.44	.45	.55	.70	.74	.54	.69	1.00					.82	-.22
Jews	.62	.44	.67	.59	.61	.62	.66	.57	1.00				.82	.17
Arabs	.46	.45	.60	.80	.82	.57	.65	.63	.66	1.00			.86	-.33
Italians	.58	.49	.65	.54	.58	.63	.67	.62	.68	.62	1.00		.81	.24
Portuguese	.55	.48	.67	.61	.64	.65	.69	.65	.68	.69	.81	1.00	.85	.13
Moslems	.45	.44	.59	.83	.82	.55	.64	.55	.62	.87	.59	.67	.85	-.36

on the allocation of feelings of fraternity, then the 'deep structure' of the two sets of measures should be quite different.

Assessment: This hypothesis of an overwhelmingly powerful civic experience effect is not confirmed. As can be seen in Table 2, both sets of measures display similar factor solutions. In both cases, only the first two principal components have eigenvalues greater than 1. These are the only principal components that we shall attempt to interpret substantively.

Hypothesis 9: If shared Canadian experience increases the degree of structure or connectedness of the measures, we should at least expect the factor solution for the second set (series B) to display a higher eigenvalue for the first principal component.

Assessment: For the first set, dealing with new immigrants, the eigenvalues of the first two principal components account for 61.4 per cent and 9.5 per cent of the variance respectively. For the second set of measures, referring to the Canadian born, the totals are 63.1 and 8.5 per cent. These differences are slight, but they are in the predicted direction and lend support to the hypothesis.

The first principal component represents an overall average comfort or fraternity level. The second component can be interpreted as a contrast between the visible minority categories and the others. The measures that load very highly on the second principal component are those dealing with Sikhs, Indo-Pakistanis, West Indian Blacks, Muslims and Arabs. (It should be noted that the Chinese category has a neutral loading on the second principal component; we shall return to this point shortly). With respect to this second component, the slightly higher percentage of the variance explained in the first set (9.5 as opposed to 8.5) indicates that the contrast between these visible minorities and the other labels is slightly more important with respect to new immigrants than with respect to the Canadian born and raised. In other words, Canadian civic experience increases the importance of the overall general rating (the first principal component) and decreases the importance of the vismin/other contrast (the second principal component). On the whole, the factor structures of the two sets of measures are very similar, and the differences between them are slight. The direction of these differences does reveal, however, that the concern with visible minorities becomes somewhat less important once respondents realize that the individuals they are being asked about are Canadian born and raised.

Discussion and Conclusion

So far we have presented and evaluated a whole string of related hypotheses concerning the way respondents process ethnic and civic cues and transform these into verbally expressed feelings of fraternity. The overall picture that emerges from this analysis is that (i) respondents value and react positively to Canadian experience, for all ethnic origins, and (ii) at the same time, they continue to be very influenced by the perceived ethnic characteristics of their fellow Canadians. The universally valued Canadian experience credential (evidenced by the near-parallelism of the lines in Figure 1, the parallelism revealed by Figure 2 and Table 1, and the near-uniform patterns in Table 2) appears to operate alongside a more particularistic set of received views about differentially-ranked ethnic categories.

In conclusion, I would like to make a few comments on how these patterns can be interpreted sociologically.

Consider the finding that the positive impact of perceived Canadian experience on feelings of fraternity is stronger for those group labels whose overall ratings are lower, as posited by hypothesis 2B and shown in Figure 1. How can this be accounted for? One factor to consider is the demographic composition of the target groups. The groups whose overall ratings are lower differ in their demographic composition from the most highly rated groups. Specifically, the groups with the lower ratings are groups with very high proportions of members born outside Canada, while the groups with high ratings have somewhat lower proportions of their members born outside Canada. The questions in both series A and series B are worded with reference to individual members of ethno-national groups. The results suggest that an individual's Canadian experience will be more important if he or she is associated with a group that has a low cumulative aggregate level of Canadian experience. Similarly, the labels for which Canadian experience makes the least difference – namely the British, French, and other European labels– are groups with a high aggregate cumulative of Canadian experience. In other words, individual credentials appear to be more important when a group's aggregate Canadian credentials are perceived as less established. This may well reflect the different degrees to which various ethnic collectivities have been successful in vesting ethnic interests in Canadian institutions, and specifically in the civic culture. In the light of this, the role of demographic composition needs to be more systematically investigated, and research is needed on the role of other factors such as group size, mean socio-economic status, geographical concentration, perceived cultural differences, and last but not least, racial prejudice. With respect to the role of the group's perceived socio-economic status, it is interesting to note that in Goldstein's related research[14] on the determinants of prestige, occupation is the most important factor, followed by ethnicity, followed by nativity. Future research is needed that incorporates an occupational cue alongside the ethnic and civic cues that have been analyzed here.

What do the patterns reported here reveal about the evolving structure of cleavages in Canadian society? Two broad comments are in order. First of all, there is very little evidence of any 'non-charter' block or 'third force' (non-French, non-British) category operating in the collective mind of the Canadian population. Looking at the whole range of groups other than the British and the French, there is great variation. European groups have high rankings, in many cases not much lower than British or French, and many visible minorities have lower rankings. This latter contrast, between the lower ranked visible minorities and all others, is far more salient than any other. The historical legacy of Canada's earlier self-image as a 'white dominion' has of course been expunged from official ideology and removed from state policy (in theory if not always in practice). These findings suggest that the ghost of the earlier long-standing white self-image is still present in public sentiments.

These findings highlight the double disadvantage faced by recent immigrants from the lowest-ranked groups: (i) relatively less fraternity is extended to their group, and (ii) the 'penalty', so to speak, for being a new arrival as opposed to Canadian-born, is appreciably greater for these groups than for immigrants from Europe. The net result, as Figure 1 shows, is that Canadians feel less comfortable with many of their fellow citizens who were Canadian-born and raised fellow citizens (those who are Sikhs, Muslims and Arabs) than they do with many recently arrived immigrants (of European origins). This points to the necessity of continued state action aimed at integrating visible minorities into the mainstream of public life and public consciousness. At the same time, the apparent upward trend over the past several decades in evaluations of several groups that were formerly ranked low,[15] notably Ukrainians, Italians, Chinese and Native Canadian Indians, does suggest that the (relatively) low fraternity scores towards Sikhs, Arabs, and Muslims may be expected to increase in the years and decades to come. This apparent upward shift in rankings over time has only been mentioned in passing in this article, and more research is needed on its determinants and correlates. Particularly noteworthy are the factor scores given here to the Chinese label, which suggest that this group is perceived as much less of a visible minority than the other visible minorities.

The second comment concerns the interplay between different types of ethnic pluralism in Canada. As mentioned, the correlations in table 2 dealing with the French label are lower than the others and behave differently. This suggests that on the whole, feelings of fraternity towards Francophones are more complex than those involving the other labels. In similar fashion, if one examines the factor analysis of the series B measures dealing with the Canadian born, including the 13 labels as well as the Native

Canadian Indian label, a further interesting result appears. In this series, the two lowest communalities are those for the French and the Native Canadian Indian labels (details not shown). This means that feelings of comfort with Francophones and with Aboriginals are less completely explained and explainable by the same general set of factors as comfort with other groups. This provides yet further confirmation for the general view that there are qualitatively distinct types of pluralism in Canada that can only with great difficulty be subsumed under a common 'ethnic' label. As Taylor[16] and Cairns[17] have pointed out, aboriginal and Quebec nationalism clearly reflect a different order of diversity than immigrant or regional diversity. Whatever their many differences, aboriginal and Quebec nationalisms are both marked by the legacy of a problematic and ambiguous collective incorporation into the Canadian state and its elusive project of shaping some sort of larger Canadian society and identity. The results reported here show that the distinctive character of these two reactive national projects is clearly visible as such in the structure of mass perceptions. (These differences are being investigated further in another paper). The aboriginal/larger society cleavage, the French/English cleavage, the Quebec/rest of Canada cleavage, and the immigrant ethnic/larger society cleavage each has its own distinct processes visibly at work and the interplay of these different processes is evident in the results just discussed. Indeed, the departures from statistical parallelism and uniformity that have been observed here pinpoint those ways in which the Canadian case displays departures from the classical model of uniform individual incorporation implicit in T.H. Marshall's initial formulation.[18]

The general patterns reported here give a preliminary sketch of the operation of fraternity-allocation processes within Canadian society. The results appear to reflect the moderate and relatively non-intrusive character of Canadian citizenship norms. Canadian nativity and childhood experience makes a difference, but the difference it makes is relative and not absolute. Canadians are more comfortable with individuals who do have Canadian experience, but they are not necessarily *un*comfortable with new arrivals whose civic experience was gained elsewhere. This point is worth emphasizing: while the lower level of fraternity extended to recently arrived immigrants is consonant with the predictions of most theoretical thinking about the nation-state, we could also hypothesize that the magnitude of the gap may well be lower in Canada than in other states. The civic culture of Canada is clearly of a mixed type, with public civic components operating alongside ethnic components, and with Canadian civic experience being universally valued even as different ethnic labels continue to be unequally valued. This is certainly in keeping with the Canadian tradition of compromise and *via media* between public and private components of social life. In more general theoretical terms, this pattern can be seen as yet another example of the way that formal equality often coexists with substantive inequality in modern societies.

These results reflect the Canadian state's acceptance of multiple loyalties, both internal and external (dual citizenship is explicitly permitted) and in fact pinpoints one of the ways these internal and external dual loaylties may be linked, namely through membership in trans-national (trans-state) ethnic categories. In many ways Canada has never fully fit the standard models of nation and state building, and its level of internal pluralism is much higher than one would expect on the basis of its high level of economic development. Canada can in fact be considered the most extreme outlier in the overall relationship between level of national development and degree of internal pluralism.[19]

The established new-world habit of using exactly the same labels for groups of born and raised Canadians as for types of foreigners and new arrivals (which would be considered very strange indeed in a country like France, for example) reinforces the idea that whatever it is that is distinctive about being Canadian coexists alongside other attributes, specifically ethnic ones, which may be shared with citizens of other states. This public use of ethnic labels, fully sanctioned by the Canadian state and nicely illustrated by the data being analyzed here, reinforces the view that 'national' differences are relative indeed. It is not surprising that this sanctioning of ethnic labels as 'natural' characteristics of Canadian citizens, explicit in many early interpretations of the multiculturalism policy, for example, has led to many calls for a corrective counter-shift in the direction of having state policies emphasize the civic elements that Canadians of all origins share and hold in common. It would be unfortunate if these appeals were to be confused with the call for the state to withdraw completely from the ethnocultural and linguistic spheres and leave everything to market forces.

This is a challenging period for building civic consciousness, when corporate identities, even those that are exalted national symbols, are becoming less clearly 'national', often with the full consent or at least passive acceptance of the state. This points to the need for research on the parallels and links between the rules governing individual and corporate citizenship in Canada. Just as 'Canadian' corporations are allowed to be part of, or be linked to, larger international conglomerates, so it is that Canadian citizens are allowed to have ties to other states, as well as to ethnonational entities that transcend state boundaries. Should this state of affairs be considered less developed and less modern, or rather is it post-modern? Both interpretations are possible, of course, which is why Canada is such a complex and stimulating society.

APPENDIX:
THE SURVEY SAMPLE

'The total sample for the 1991 Multiculturalism and Canadians Survey involved a base sample of 2,500 Canadian adults along with 'booster' samples in each of Toronto, Montreal and Vancouver in order to include at least 500 respondents in each of the three major urban centres in Canada. The total augmented sample was 3325.

Telephone numbers for the sample were randomly generated using the Angus Reid Group in-house computerized sample selection procedure which generates telephone numbers randomly by census division such that the sample is selected proportionate to population distributions consistent with Census data. A quota system was used to ensure proportionate representation by male and female respondents.

The survey was administered by telephone through the Angus Reid Group's national network of eight telephone interviewing centres across Canada. All telephone interviewing was conducted between June 29th and July 17th 1991. Interviews were conducted in either English or French, according to the language preference of the respondent.'

Source: Angus Reid Group, *Multiculturalism and Canadians: National Attitude Survey 1991*, report submitted to Multiculturalism and Citizenship Canada, August 1991.

NOTES

The author is indebted to the Policy and Research Directorate of Multiculturalism and Citizenship Canada for making these data available for secondary analysis. Responsibility for the analyses reported here lies with the author alone, and neither Multiculturalism and Citizenship Canada (now the Department of Canadian Heritage) nor the Angus Reid Group is responsible for the analyses reported here. An earlier version of this article was presented at the Biennial Conference of the Canadian Ethnic Studies Association in Vancouver in November 1993. The author would also like to thank Jean Laponce and the other Ottawa roundtable participants for their helpful comments.

1. The working definition of Canadian society being used here is a pragmatic operational one, encompassing all activities occuring within the political and territorial boundaries of the Canadian state. On the problematic meaning of the terms nation, state, society, and country in the Canadian context, see Claude Denis, 'Quebec-as-distinct-society as Conventional Wisdom: The Constitutional Silence of Anglo-Canadian Sociologists', *Canadian Journal of Sociology*, Vol.18, No.3, 1993.
2. See for example Michael T. Hannan and John Meyer (eds.), *National Development and the World System* (Chicago: University of Chicago Press, 1979)
3. Immanuel Wallerstein, *The Capitalist World Economy* (New York: Cambridge University Press, 1979). William H. McNeill, *Polyethnicity and National Unity in World History* (Toronto: University of Toronto Press, 1986). Eric Hobsbawm, *Nations and Nationalism since 1780: Programme, Myth, Reality* (New York: Cambridge University Press, 1990).
4. Ursula Vogel and Michael Moran, 'Introduction', in Ursula Vogel and Michael Moran (eds.), *The Frontiers of Citizenship* (New York: St. Martin's Press, 1991), p.xii.
5. See for example Dominique Schnapper, *La France de l'intégration: sociologie de la nation en 1990* (Paris: Gallimard, 1991).
6. Anthony D. Smith, *Theories of Nationalism* (New York: Harper and Row, 1971).
7. Philip Resnick, *The Masks of Proteus: Reflections on the Canadian and Modern State* (Montreal and Kingston: McGill-Queen's University Press, 1990). Raymond Breton, 'From Ethnic to Civic Nationalism: English Canada and Quebec', *Ethnic and Racial Studies*, Vol.11, No.1, 1988.
8. John W. Berry, Rudolf Kalin and Donald M. Taylor, *Multiculturalism and Ethnic Attitudes in Canada*, (Ottawa: Supply and Services Canada, 1977).
9. Peter Pineo, 'The Social Standing of Ethnic and Racial Groupings in Canada', *Canadian*

Review of Sociology and Anthropology, Vol.14, 1977, p.147–57

10. Reginald W. Bibby, 'Bilingualism and Multiculturalism: A National Reading', in Leo Driedger (ed.), *Ethnic Canada:Identities and Inequalites*, (Toronto: Copp Clark Pitman, 1987).

11. Jay Goldstein, 'The Influence of Ethnicity, Occupation, and Nativity on Social Standing: Some Western Canadian Data', *Canadian Ethnic Studies* Vol.20 No.1, 1988, p.66–77

12. Ibid.

13. Philip Converse, 'The Nature of Belief Systems in Mass Publics', in David Apter (ed.), *Ideology and Discontent* (New York: Free Press, 1964), p.206–261.

14. Goldstein, 1988.

15. See Pineo 1977 and Berry, Kalin and Taylor 1977.

16. Charles Taylor, *Rapprocher les solitudes* (Québec: Presses de l'Université Laval, 1992).

17. Alan C. Cairns, 'Canada's Fragmented Citizenship', in William Kaplan (ed.), *Belonging: The Meaning and Future of Canadian Citizenship* (Montreal and Kingston: McGill-Queen's University Press, 1993).

18. See Vogel and Moran 1991.

19. Leslie S. Laczko, 'Canada's Pluralism in Comparative Perspective', *Ethnic and Racial Studies*, Vol.17 No.1, 1994, p.20–41

Ethnicities, Citizenship and Feminisms: Theorizing the Political Practices of Intersectionality

CAROLINE ANDREW

This article explores the present state of theorizing about the political practices of the intersections of feminisms and ethnicity. This particular question raises the larger question of the political practices of difference, or the ways the intersections of multiple identities can be translated into political practice. The article looks first at the way in which this issue has emerged, both from the political practice of the Canadian women's movement and from the intellectual challenge of postmodernism. Following a brief examination of Canadian feminist writings on the analysis of intersections of gender and ethnicity, the text looks at the political practices of intersectionality through the question of citizenship and the relationship between the public and private spheres. Although some interesting arguments are to be found in the literature about the potential for the development of coalition politics that take account of difference but also of common citizenship, it is not at all clear that this will be the direction that will be taken by the politics of the women's movement in Canada.

Introduction

This article is a very preliminary effort to explore the theorizing of the political practices of the intersections of feminism and ethnicity. The pluralizing of ethnicity and feminism in the title is central to the argument that the relationship between feminism and ethnicity has brought to the forefront the question of the diversity of identities – therefore, ethnicities and feminisms. The real question being theorized is the political practices of difference, or the ways in which the intersections of multiple identities can be translated into political practice.

My particular approach to the analysis of the intersections of ethnicity and feminism is to examine how feminist theory has looked at the relationship between feminism and ethnicity. My intention is to give equal theoretical weight to ethnicity and feminism, but my intellectual standpoint is from feminist theory to the theorizing of ethnicity. Parallel to this, my political standpoint is similar; as a participant in women's groups (particularly the Canadian Research Institute for the Advancement of

Women, at the national level, and the Women's Action Centre against Violence (Ottawa-Carleton) at the local level) where questions relating to the political practices of difference have been central. However, the positions put forward in this text are entirely my personal reflections and do not reflect the position of either of these two organizations.

The political practices being theorized here are those of the Canadian women's movement. Once again, the intention is to give equal weight to considerations of ethnicity and of feminism but the fact that it is the practices of the women's movement and therefore the practices of ethnicity as they relate to women's groups does give a particular cast to the analysis.

The Emerging Issue: the Context of Political Practices

Issues of difference and diversity are central questions of present-day politics. 'Horizontal hostilities',[1] debates about current exclusionary practices and demands for inclusion based on ethnicity and on race, are high on the Canadian political agenda. These debates have been particularly salient within the Canadian women's movement. The challenge, both intellectual and practical, of understanding, exploring, and managing diversity is now clear to the feminist movement. Although there is certainly debate on the specific analysis to be made of the exclusionary nature of white bourgeois feminism in Canada, the challenge about diversity and about multiple identities is now a central issue (Agnew, 1993; Stasiulis, 1990; Bannerji, 1987; Dhruvarajan, 1991; Medjuck, 1990).

Simply considering the intersections of feminism and ethnicity is, indeed, inadequate. The question of difference, or multiple identities, is more complex. It involves the intersections of gender, ethnicity, class, language, sexual orientation, age, able bodiedness and so on. It also involves an uneasiness about simply putting these factors in a neat hierarchical order and a corresponding insistence that each must be treated as important, both politically and theoretically. However thinking about feminism and ethnicity, or rather the intersections of feminisms and ethnicities, is the best way into this larger question. It is the simultaneous recognition of gender and ethnicity that has, rather like the collision of two stars, led to a stunning, exhilarating and almost cataclismic fragmentation of identities. The recognition of these specific fragmentations has been the most salient politically, with class as the perennially less visible definer of political position and political practice in Canada.

The question of the ordering, or not, of the various factors that make up the multiple identities is a complex one, both theoretically and practically. On the one hand, there is a recognition that not all these factors relate to categories that are oppressed in Canadian society. The categories of being white, or able bodied or heterosexual are associated with social status, and therefore analyses, to be accurate, must take into account questions of structural inequality and the recognition of double or triple disadvantage. On the other hand, there are various forms of resistance to creating a hierarchy of oppression, notably a concern that this will lead to pointless discussions about the specific order of oppressions. (Are First Nations women more disadvantaged than women with disabilities? And what about First Nations women with disabilities?) There is also a concern that the ordering of inequality is a way of silencing certain women and that there must be a way of allowing the experience of each individual woman to be recognized. These concerns arise on the theoretical level but even more so, on the level of political practice.

And, indeed, the focus of this article is not the theorizing of the intersections of gender and ethnicity, but rather the theorizing of the political practice of these intersections. This is so in part because my entry to this question stems from practical politics but also because I believe that theoretically the most urgent question to understand is that of political practice. I am not therefore talking about the way people live the intersections of ethnicity and gender (in which case, the analysis of the role of the family and other primary social groups would be of more importance) but rather about the way women have organized themselves politically in relation to these intersections.

This is not to suggest that there is no relation between the way people live the intersections of ethnicity and gender and questions of political organization but rather that they are not identical questions. The choice of organizations through which one chooses to act politically imposes definitions of identity that strengthen certain identities and suppress others. A feminist who is an immigrant woman with a disability might choose to be active in the National Organization of Immigrant and Visible Minority Women (NOIVM) or in the Disabled Women's Network (DAWN) or in a local group providing services to pre-school aged children (just three out of an almost unlimited number of choices). Each of these organizational choices would highlight different elements of the participant's identity. Each of the choices would reflect in part an explicit decision on the part of the participant but the decision is influenced by the reality of which groups exist in a particular context. Political practice reflects both the efforts of individual political actors and the impact of the organizational context.

It is a matter of some urgency to think about these questions of practice in a theoretical way, to formulate abstractions of reality and to see how these help to address the practical issues. My experience with the practical politics of the intersections of race, class and gender is that theory is extraordinarily important. The way people react is linked not only to their emotions or to the specific situation but also to the vision they have of the relationships between ideas; being conceptually clear about situations helps people to understand relationships and enables them to use this understanding to guide their behaviour. Nothing is so practical as a good theory, and for this reason I would argue that the most practical step ahead for the politics of diversity in Canada is to attempt to theorize these politics.

Theoretical Conceptualization and the Emerging Issue

The questions about intersectionality emerge from political reality. At the same time it is clear that these questions also emerge from changing modes of conceptualization. Postmodernism has given visibility to fragmentation, marginalization and multiple identities. The central question in this article – how to theorize the intersections of feminisms and ethnicities – is in part a reflection of postmodern sensibilities.

Postmodernism is certainly an important intellectual step towards the reconceptualizing of difference. The idea of multiple, fluid identities, of things being both what they are and what they are not, of the end of meganarrative – all these open up the debate for the better understanding of difference. However, at the same time as postmodernism sharpens the analysis of the intersections of gender and ethnicity, it also blunts, if not distorts, this analysis. As Seyla Benhabib states in her analysis of feminism and postmodernism, a strong version of postmodernism 'would undermine the very possibility of feminism as the theoretical articulation of the emancipatory aspirations of women.'[2] Her analysis is that the central tenets of postmodernism; the death of Man, of History and of Metaphysics, can be understood in both a weak and a strong way; the weak way opens up a greater number of social interpretations, whereas the strong form of postmodernism is the denial of any logic to the relations between these social interpretations. The weak version may offer interesting possibilities to feminists, but the strong version of postmodernism is not compatible with feminism.

This relationship is an important one to explore, with the sense of promise – and also deception – involved in relating postmodernism and feminism. The importance of multiplicity, particularity and marginality; the pleasures of ambiguity, paradox and contradiction; the refusal of meganarrative and the triumphant celebration of 'contingent, historically changing and culturally variable social, linguistic and discursive practices'[3] – all these are apparent in the ways in which the importance of recognizing difference within the feminist movement became increasingly visible.

At the same time reading these manifestations only through a postmodern lens is reductionist and perhaps worse. The call to recognize difference, and more specifically the recognition of ethnicity and race, is not only to recognize a more varied set of discursive practices but even more to recognize racism and discrimination and to build an inclusive political practice.

Thinking about the relationship between feminist theory and postmodernism does open up the question of what a major intellectual step it is to attempt the conceptualization of difference and particularly the simultaneous recognition of the non-hierarchized intersections of multiple differences. Until recently almost all our theorizing was about one difference, or about comparisons between groups who differed along only one dimension. Nitya Iyer gives an eloquent description of this thinking. She argues that 'the model upon which each type of discrimination doctrine is based is someone who diverges from the norm in only one respect − a white (adult, able − bodied and so on) woman in a sex discrimination case, a racial minority man in a race discrimination case.'[4] Her conclusion is to argue for complexity.

> It is true such an approach is a call for what might appear to be an intimidating degree of complexity, with a corresponding diminution in our confidence in the correctness of decisions, our shared belief that the tribunal 'got it right,' and that justice was done. But without complexity and the uncertainty it brings, the justice we claim is only justice for some... For racial minority women and for others who straddle the current categories of difference, complicating our human rights law in the ways I have suggested is not one of several options for reform. It is the only way not to disappear.[5]

This is not to excuse past generations of scholars, nor the mainstream Canadian women's movement for their neglect of an adequately complex theorization of the intersections of ethnicity and feminism, but rather to underline the dramatically different level of difficulty involved in the conceptualization of multiple identities. Moving from considering single categories − women/men, black/white or even liberal feminism/socialist feminism/radical feminism − to reflecting on the intersections of even two equally important categories and, more importantly, three or four equally important categories, is a quantum step in complexity.

Despite acknowledging this complexity, it is surprising that it has taken us so long in Canada to arrive at theorizing intersectionality. Although the current categorization of Canada as the first postmodern country is in part a question of fashion, it does reflect the persistence of numerous levels of reality, each of which is inescapable, or 'incontournable', in political terms. Even a simple study of regionalism, coexisting with francophone-anglophone differences calls for an analysis of intersectionality, but add in a recognition of the importance of the relationship between indigenous people and the white settlers of the northern half of North America, plus the feminist perspective of the importance of a gendered analysis – all these suggest an awareness of the importance of intersectionality in Canadian life that should have been translated clearly into our intellectual tradition.

The Treatment of Intersections in Canadian Feminist Writings

What has been the record of Canadian feminist writings in considering the intersections of gender with other social factors? Our treatment here is by no means a thorough analysis of this question but rather a broad overview of certain themes and certain types of analysis. By this we hope to get some sense of areas that have been covered and areas in which little has been done.

There has been an important Canadian tradition of reflection on the intersections of gender and class (Armstrong and Armstrong, 1984; Hamilton and Barrett, 1987; Maroney and Luxton, 1987; Armstrong and Connelly, 1989). This stems both from the importance of the practice of socialist feminism and of the intellectual tradition of political economy. The early work in this area, as, for example, the domestic labour debate and the debate stemming from the Armstrongs' article on 'Beyond Sexless Class and Classless Sex',[6] was often theoretical and/or general in its intent and in its argument. The intellectual objective was to understand how feminism and Marxism (or Marxism and feminism) could be put together or to see how the insights of both could be combined.

There is also a body of material in Canada that has looked at the intersections of gender and ethnicity. The 1981 special issue of *Canadian Ethnic Studies* on 'Ethnicity and Femininity' illustrates the early material in this area. Once again, this material is often general and/or theoretical in approach, with the intent of analyzing themes of 'subordination and powerlessness'[7] and of analyzing the interrelationships between the social construction of gender and of ethnicity. At the same time material is presented that relates to very concrete examples of social construction, as for example Roxana Ng's description of immigrant women. 'The ethnicity of an immigrant woman arises in, and only in, a set of social relations which articulates her experience to the society that surrounds her, of which she is a part'.[8] The growing interest in producing highly contextualized and contingent material in part reflects the influence of Dorothy Smith's work on daily life and indeed it is significant to note that the special issue of *Canadian Ethnic Studies* was dedicated jointly to Jean Burnet and to Dorothy Smith.

It is also important to note the concern of almost all the articles in this special issue with the intersections not only of gender and ethnicity but also of class. Juteau and Roberts describe 'three systems of domination',[9] including gender, ethnicity and class. This triple lens is a strong theme throughout the issue.

There has been less material produced on the intersections between gender and some of the other highly important identities (CRIAW, 1993). Work on sexual orientation and gender is beginning to emerge (for example, *Resources for Feminist Research* 1983, Stone 1991) while material on gender and disability is an even more recent phenomenon (*Resources for Feminist Research* 1985, *Canadian Women Studies* 1993, Stewart, Percival and Epperly 1992). This work in general incorporates ethnicity, as well as class, along with gender.

The more recent material on ethnicity and gender tends to look at these intersections within highly particularized examples of the social construction of identity. Part of this comes from the recognition that place, and space, are part of the formative elements of identity. Jenson's analysis of the 'universe of political discourse'[10] represents one method of integrating the role of individual actors and historical specificity within the impact of broad structural factors. This offers the possibility of at least including the self-representation of social actors and therefore seeing how particular intersections are perceived by those actors.

In this vein, there have been a growing number of studies that look at particular cases of the social construction of identities that include gender, ethnicity, class and, more generally, that look at the construction of multiple identities. Examples are Cardinal (1992), Ng (1988), Parr (1990) and Iacovetta (1992). Cardinal looks at Franco-ontarian women, Ng looks at immigrant women in the context of a service agency relating to employment questions, Parr looks at workers in two Ontario towns and Iacovetta looks at 'the encounter between social workers and their immigrant clients'.[11] All of these studies indicate a sensitivity to difference, to the constitution of multiple identities through the highly particularized working out of the intersections of gender, ethnicity, class and many other factors.

> Never did class and gender, either simply or in conjunction, map the whole of social existence; both personally and collectively, understandings and obligations were also framed in religious faith, ethnicity and nationality. None of these roles was assumed separately... The simultaneity of these ways of being was inescapable, and from this simultaneity followed heterogeneity.[12]

The hierarchization of the different factors are highly contingent on the specific context being described. In a particular case, one factor may be more pertinent than others but, overall, the analyses are more concerned with understanding a multiplicity of factors.

Recently, there is a growing literature which looks at the social construction of identities in the political sphere and which has given particular attention to the ways in which the women's movement has integrated, or not, the intersections of gender and ethnicity. Some of this material focuses on the inclusion, or lack thereof, of race within Canadian feminist organizing (Agnew, 1993; Bannerji, 1987; Dhruvarajan, 1991), whereas others look at a set of factors, such as gender, race, class and sexual orientation (Adamson, Briskin, McPhail, 1988) or gender, race, ethnicity and class (Stasiulis, 1990). These studies also include the work done on rereading the first wave of Canadian feminism, in order to deconstruct what is seen as its racism (Valverde, 1992). In general, this material is highly critical of the inability and/or the refusal of the Canadian women's movement to integrate, in a non-hierarchized way, the components of multiple identities, be they ethnicity, race, disability, sexual orientation and/or age.

This rather long parenthesis on the treatment of intersections in Canadian feminist writings allows for an acknowledgement of the important work that has been done as well as a recognition of the fact that much remains to be done. Certain intersections have been better explored than others, and much recent literature deals with issues that relate directly to the central question of this article, how to theorize the political practices of intersectionality.

The Politics of Position and Personal Responsibility

In trying to advance our understanding of the political practices of intersectionality I am doing so through an admittedly partial, and idiosyncratic, reading of feminist theorists' writing on politics, particularly on democracy and on citizenship, and these writers are preoccupied with questions of diversity.

A first set of remarks builds on the recognition of multiple identities and calls for action based on clear thinking about the complexities of intersectionality. Examples of this can be seen in Pratt and Hanson's discussion of 'critical self-examination and personal responsibility'[13] or in the editorial in *Environment and Planning D: Society and Space* (Jackson, 1991) which advocates 'a more clearly articulated politics of position, by which I mean not just those positions that we choose to adopt but also the multiple ways in which we are positioned'.[14] The editorial goes on to state that:

A politics of position, articulated along these lines, accepts that there are no definite or disinterested answers to the current crisis of representation. But, equally, it rejects the most extreme forms of cultural relativism and argues that it is only possible to enter such debates from a particular position, conscious of the extent to which that position is empowering or disempowering.[15]

That this is both a theoretical and a practical question is clear. As a white middle class woman, for me to act politically requires having the theoretical tools to be able to reflect on the simultaneous influence of my race, my language, my class and my gender, but it also requires that I am willing to examine those parts of my identity that represent domination and/or exclusion. I have to be willing to think about my whiteness and its consequences, about the privileges of being middle-class, about the dominant status of English in Canada, about the way ability influences privilege, and so on. For me, and for us collectively, this has not been easy – and the difficulties are as much theoretical as practical. The above overview of the literature indicates that analysis of intersectionality is much less frequent that the analysis of one form of discrimination and/or oppression. For many white middle-class women their political identity is as women and their principal political position is one of felt discrimination, if not oppression, in the society. It is clear that it is not easy to rethink this hugely important single identity and to understand it as much more multiple and many layered. This is all the harder when, in practical terms, the additional levels of identity have an entirely different relation to the world in terms of power. One may be disempowered as a woman, but empowered as white and as middle-class.

I have emphasized the theoretical difficulties of this kind of politics of position although I also believe that there are real and important practical reasons why this recognition has been difficult. I do this in part because I feel that the theoretical reasons have not always been given enough importance. For example, it requires tools of conceptualization to understand that the recognition of sets of differences does not imply that one is dismissing any single one of these differences as unimportant, or to think of multiple oppressions in a way that combines structure and contingency. These can be brought home through practical situations but they are inherently theoretical, or methodological, questions. Jeannie Martin makes this point in her article on 'Multiculturalism and Feminism'. Having criticized multiculturalism theorists for their exclusion of women, she indicates that feminism must also be challenged for its ethnocentricism.

> This raises issues for mainstream (dominant) feminism concerning assumptions about the universal (general-normal) female and the particular (specific – deviant, other) female. As Anglo feminists are

clearly situated in a position of ethnic domination, it should be apparent that inattention to these questions perpetuates, not feminism, but ethnic (or racial) and male domination.

Criticisms are easy, solutions are not... Overall the issue seems partly an issue about methodology, at least as it has been discussed in this paper. For example, in the Australian case, methodological 'do-nots' that arise from the foregoing analysis include: do not employ a method that compares oppressions; do not attempt to find out 'about' migrant women, (to pose the question this immediately positions migrant women 'out there' to be investigated as different from 'us' and calls them to account accordingly); do not pose feminist questions via two-sided formulas (for example universal and particular, public and private, women and the family... and class, and the state, and...). Rather assume that what is female is situated fluidly, ambiguously and variously in the space between each side, and accept that a feminist account proceeds from here.[16]

The quotation is long but important because it restates, with specific examples, the stages involved in moving from thinking about an oppression to thinking about the intersections of the multiple dimensions of reality.

These clarifications about the politics of position are both highly significant and, at the same time, relatively limited in their application to the practices of politics. They are useful, and indeed even important, to the attitudes one takes and to the ethical forming of one's political position but they do not really speak to the way politics goes on – to the practices of politics.

The Practices of Politics and the Nature of Citizenship

Trying to understand political practice leads us to the question of the relationship of the various actors to their political community. For Chantal Mouffe, this leads directly to the question of citizenship.

The question at stake is to make the fact that we belong to different communities of races, language, culture and others compatible with our common belonging to a political community whose rules we have to accept. As against conceptions that stress commonality at the expense of plurality and respect of differences or that deny any form of commonality in the name of plurality and difference, what we need is to envisage a form of commonality that respects diversity and makes room for different forms of individuality. I believe that the crux of the problem lies in the way we conceptualize the political community and the way in which we belong to the political community, that is, citizenship.[17]

Another dimension of this question of the political community is to focus on the 'political' and to see how this has been constructed in terms of the relationship between the public and private spheres. Citizenship belongs to the public sphere and therefore the way in which each society has constructed the private and the public is fundamental to the recognition of multiple identities.

Jean Bethke Elshtain's 1993 Massey Lectures, *Democracy on Trial* deals with this in her analysis of what she calls 'a politics of displacement'.[18] By this she means politics in which every dimension of private life is seen as legitimately public and at the same time, everything that is public is privatized in its treatment and interpretation. Elshtain continues: 'This merging of the public and private is anathema to democratic thinking, which holds that the distinction between public and private identities, commitments, and activities is of vital importance'.[19]

Her examples of the politics of displacement all relate to gender and ethnicity. 'For persons thus identified the category of 'citizen' is a matter of indifference at best; contempt at worst. More and more we see ourselves in exclusive terms along racial or gender or sexual preference lines. If this is who I am, why should I care about the citizen?'[20] Except that I would substitute 'along racial *and* gender *and* sexual preference lines', Elshtain is clearly identifying a real phenomenon. Her analysis – that the 'personal is political' is not understood as meaning that the 'personal and political are interrelated in important and fascinating ways previously hidden by sexist ideology and practice, nor that the personal and political may be analogous to each other along certain axes of power and privilege'[21] but literally that the personal and the political are identical – does illustrate the approach taken by some currents of feminism. And indeed the recognition of the multiplication of intersections is often accompanied by an increasingly personal account of one's relationship to politics and to political practice. The earlier quotation from Mouffe identifies this as denying 'any form of commonality in the name of plurality and difference'.[22]

However, this reading of the loss of the public sphere through the increasing acceptance of the politics of identity needs to be juxtaposed to the criticism of those who define the public sphere in such a way that it excludes all but an extremely narrow norm. If Elshtain identifies the crisis in democracy with the mindless behaviour of those who eliminate the public sphere by arguing only the personal, others argue that the crisis is as much from the behaviour of those who stultify the public sphere by defining it in such narrow and rigid ways as to exclude most, if not all, emancipatory politics. Iris Marion Young argues for a heterogenous public sphere, asserting that 'the only way to ensure that public life will not exclude persons and groups which it has excluded in the past is to give special recognition to the disadvantage of these groups and bring their specific histories into the public'.[23] Gender and race are specifically identified by Young as her discussion of past exclusion identifies 'women and racialized groups culturally identified with the body, wildness and irrationality'.[24] Young is, like Elshtain, arguing for a revitalized public sphere but her argument is that this must be on new grounds and that the distinction between public and private must not be 'an opposition between reason and affectivity and desire, or universal and particular'.[25] In other words, for Young the distinction must not be used simply to continue to exclude groups from public participation and public power. This is similar to Chantal Mouffe's position which acknowledges the emancipatory potential of the demands of a variety of social movements. Her argument is based upon

> ... a concept of citizenship that, through a common identification with a radical democratic interpretation of the principles of liberty and equality, aims at constructing a 'we', a claim of equivalence among their demands so as to articulate them through the principle of democratic equivalence.[26]

Anne Phillips, in *Engendering Democracy*, also discusses this question. She argues for the importance of distinguishing between public and private spheres and acknowledges that feminism has not always been clear on this.

> Though feminism is often hijacked by those who dissolve differences of scale and kind into a disturbingly amorphous mess, there are crucial distinctions between being a citizen and being a nice caring person... 'The democratization of everyday life' is thus fair enough as a slogan that captures the importance of democratic equality in every sphere of human existence. It is misleading if it denies all distinction between politics and everyday life.[27]

Phillips calls for a recognition of the public sphere and 'citizen values' but also for a widening of the spheres in society in which an increased democratization is necessary. 'Feminism multiplies the places within which democracy appears relevant, and then it alters the dimensions as well. 'Details matter.'[28] Her argument is for a 'mixed-economy'[29] that combines a variety of forms of democracy – liberal democracy, participatory democracy and civic republicanism.

Both Young and Phillips call for the recognition of collective identities within the public sphere. For Phillips,

Feminists are surely right to argue that people should not have to leave their sexual identities behind when they climb on to the political stage. But neither should they have to define themselves by one criterion, in this case by gender, alone.[30]

Indeed, Phillips ends her book by arguing that 'we have to find a political language that can recognize heterogeneity and difference, but does not thereby capitulate to an essentialism that defines each of us by one aspect alone'.[31]

Young makes an argument for the importance of group representation as a means to the repoliticization of public life. She argues that the ideal of universal citizenship is in fact a way of maintaining privileged groups in power. Groups that speak for the oppressed or the disadvantaged should be recognized because identification with these groups is an important factor for the political mobilization of their members. It is only with the recognition of these groups in the public sphere that 'commitment to the need and desire to decide together the society's policies fosters communication across those differences'.[32] An inclusive political practice must develop through the institutionalized recognition of group representation, where those groups act for the oppressed or the disadvantaged. Young details the kind of institutional mechanisms and public resources that she is talking about; these should support the self-organization of group members, allow them to develop and present social policy proposals and, finally, have veto power over specific policies affecting them. One could argue that the Canadian state has, at least in part, followed this model. In the post war period, public resources in Canada have been allocated to the self-organization of certain groups acting for the oppressed and the disadvantaged (certainly not all groups, and there are questions about levels of support, and vital questions recently about whether this practice has ended or is about to end). On a number of occasions, public resources have been made available to allow groups to organize and present policy proposals (again the same questions can be asked about which groups have been supported and, particularly, about what is likely to happen to this in the near future). Despite these questions, it is clear that there has been state support for the organization of groups representing the disadvantaged. Certainly the Women's Programme of the federal government has been a major factor in giving resources to women's groups, and multicultural groups have been supported in the same way. The Canadian example could be seen therefore to follow the first two of the three forms of institutional mechanisms described by Young. The third level, veto power over policies effecting these groups, has not been true in the Canadian context.

But, of course, it is the issue of veto power that is central in relation to political practice and this raises questions about the ways in which group recognition can take place. The issues of public resources for organization and for input can be seen as indications of the society's claims to equality and the will towards inclusion (as well as that of the level of public resources available) but the question of veto power involves more directly the ways in which the groups must relate to one another and to the whole society, in terms not only of process but of final decisions.

One of the problems raised by the question of veto power relates directly to the political consequences of the simultaneous recognition of the intersections of multiple dimensions of reality: the increasingly numerous and increasingly specific character of the groups. Indeed, it is interesting to look at the groups identified by Young (in the American context): 'Women, blacks, Native Americans, Chicanos, Puerto Ricans and other Spanish-speaking Americans, Asian Americans, gay men, lesbians, working-class people, poor people, old people, and mentally and physically disabled people'.[33] With the exception of the distinction between gay men and lesbians, each of these groups is categorized in terms of only one oppression or exclusion, but if we are talking about the political mobilization of real groups, this is not current reality. One is less likely to be talking about a group representing people with disabilities and more likely to be talking about lesbian visible-minority women with disabilities arguing that they being silenced in an organization representing visible-minority women with disabilities.

Young does recognize that multiple identities exist and that 'every group has group differences cutting across it',[34] but this is a somewhat simplistic way of understanding current politics. The intersections are more likely to be between groups than within groups, and this changes political practice. It raises questions about the way in which group recognition could play itself out in the political sphere. It suggests that our concern for the theorizing of the political practices of intersectionality should look at ways that deal not only with the internal functioning of groups and their relation to the political sphere, but also with the relationships of groups to each other in the political sphere.

Towards a Definition of Coalition Politics

A suggestive channel of thought is that raised by Seyla Benhabib. She identifies what she considers to be two strains of communitarian political thought, an integrationist strain and a participatory one. A link can be made between these two strains and two possible ways of acting in terms of the intersections of feminism and ethnicity: through a preoccupation for the content of the differences or through a preoccupation with the process of acting in relation to the whole. The integrationist strain wants to solve the problems of individualism and anomie of modern society through the recovery of some coherent value scheme, whereas the participationist thread 'sees the problems of modernity less in the loss of a sense of belonging, oneness and solidarity but more in the sense of a loss of political agency and efficacy'.[35] For Benhabib, the participatory thread does not involve dedifferentiation or value homogeneity: 'the public sentiment which is encouraged is not reconciliation and harmony, but rather political agency and efficacy, namely the sense that we have a say in the economic, political and civic arrangements that define our lives together, and that what one does make a difference'.[36]

This description suggests a basis for working together that is grounded in a recognition of difference and differentiation. It is based on the sharing of a political project but it directs itself, not to the substantive goals, but to agreement on the processes of working towards that political project. Indeed, this avenue is similar to that proposed by Mouffe or by Young. All three are talking about forms of coalition that relate to democratic citizenship and that permit the working together across differences. Young talks of the ideal of a 'rainbow coalition'[37] and Mouffe of 'the experience of a radical and plural democracy' consisting 'in the recognition of the multiplicity of social logics along with the necessity of their articulation'.[38] There would seem to be a shared agreement on the importance of citizenship-based coalition politics.

But, despite the interest of this possibility, it seems unlikely to succeed, given the current strength for the integrationist strain. When Benhabib describes this strain as one that 'emphasizes value revival, value reform, or value regeneration and rejects institutional solutions',[39] she identifies many of the themes of modern identity politics. The emphasis on personal values tends to lead to increasingly precise and narrow, not to say exclusive, definitions of the group that holds those particular values.

So, too, with the political project. The desire to regroup people on the basis of increasingly complex intersections can lead to more and more specific political projects that are pertinent only to the members of the group.Therefore, despite being intrigued by the directions suggested by Benhabib, Mouffe, and Young and optimistic about the possibilities for the political practices of diversity that these open up, I am relatively pessimistic about the likelihood that these directions will be followed. This pessimism does not however negate the importance of continuing the efforts at theorization. The challenge of theorizing the political practices of difference, and particularly the intersections of ethnicities and feminisms remains both a theoretical and a practical priority.

NOTES

The author would like to thank Alan Cairns, Linda Cardinal and Michèle Kerisit for their useful comments on the preliminary version of this article.

1. Geraldine Pratt and Susan Hanson, 'Geography and the Construction of Difference', *Gender, Place and Culture*, Vol.1 No.1 p.12.
2. Seyla Benhabib, *Situating the Self: Gender, Community and Postmodernism in Contemporary Ethics* (New York: Routledge, 1992), p.229.
3. Ibid., p.212.
4. Nitya Iyer, 'Disappearing Women: Racial Minority Women in Human Rights Cases', *Canadian Journal of Women and the Law*, Vol.6, No.1, p.42.
5. Ibid., p.51.
6. Roberta Hamilton and Michèle Barrett, *The Politics of Diversity: Feminism Marxism and Nationalism* (Montreal: Book Centre Inc., 1987), pp.208–240.
7. Danielle Juteau and Barbara Roberts, 'Special Issue: Ethnicity and Femininity', *Canadian Ethnic Studies*, Vol.8, No.1, p.vii.
8. Roxana Ng, 'Constructing Ethnic Phenomenon', *Canadian Ethnic Studies*, Vol.8, No.1, p.103.
9. Danielle Juteau and Barbara Roberts, 'Ethnicity and Femininity: d'après nos expériences', *Canadian Ethnic Studies*, Vol.8, No.1, p.7.
10. Jane Jenson, 'Gender and Reproduction, or Babies and the State', *Studies in Political Economy*, No.20, pp.9–46
11. Franco Iacovetta, 'Making New Canadians: Social Workers, Women and the Reshaping of Immigrant Families', in Franca Iacovetta and Mariana Valverde, *Gender Conflicts* (Toronto: University of Toronto Press, 1992), p.264.
12. Joy Parr, *the Gender of Breadwinners* (Toronto: University of Toronto Press, 1990), p.245.
13. Pratt and Hanson, p.7
14. P.Jackson, 'Guest Editorial', *Environment and Planning D: Society and Space*, Vol.9, p.131.
15. Ibid., p.133.
16. Jeannie Martin, 'Multiculturalism and Feminism', in Gill Bottomley et al, *Intersexions: gender, class, culture, ethnicity* (North Sydney: Allen and Unwin, 1991), p.131.
17. Chantal Mouffe, 'Citizenship and Political Identity', *October*, No.61, p.30.
18. Jean Bethke Elshtain, *Democracy on Trial* (Concord: Anansi, 1993), p.38.
19. Ibid., p.36.
20. Ibid., p.4.
21. Ibid., pp.42–43.
22. Mouffe, p.30.
23. Iris Marion Young, ' Impartiality and the Civic Public', in Seyla Benhabib and Drucilla Cornell, *Feminism as Critique* (London: Polity Press, 1987), p.76.
24. Ibid., p.73.
25. Ibid.
26. Mouffe, p.31
27. Anne Phillips, *Engendering Democracy* (University Park: The Pennsylvania State University Press, 1991), pp.160–161.
28. Ibid., p.159.
29. Ibid., p.163.
30. Ibid., p.156.
31. Ibid., p.168.
32. Iris Marion Young, 'Polity and Group Difference: A Critique of the Ideal of Universal Citizenship', *Ethics*, Vol.99, No.2, p.258.
33. Ibid., p.265.
34. Ibid, p.
35. Benhabib, p.77.
36. Ibid., p.81.
37. Young, *Ethics*, p.284.

38. Mouffe, p.32.
39. Benhabib, p.77.

REFERENCES

Nancy Adamson, Linda Briskin and Margaret McPhail, *Feminist Organizing for Change* (Toronto: Oxford University Press, 1988).

Vijay Agnew, 'Canadian Feminism and Women of Colour', *Women's Studies International Forum*, Vol.16, No.3, pp.217–227.

Pat Armstrong and Hugh Armstrong, *The Double Ghetto* (Toronto: McClelland and Stewart, 1984).

Pat Armstrong and Pat Connelly, 'Feminism and Political Economy', *Studies in Political Economy*, No.30.

Himani Bannerji, 'Introducing Racism: Notes towards an Anti-Racist Feminism', *Resources for Feminist Research*, Vol.16, No.1, pp.10–12.

Seyla Benhabib, *Situating the Self: Gender, Community and Postmodernism in Contemporary Ethics* (New York: Routledge, 1992).

Canadian Research Institute on the Advancement of Women (CRIAW), *Canadian Women Studies/Feminist Research* (Ottawa: Government of Canada, 1993).

Canadian Women Studies, 'Women and Disability', 1993, pp.13–4.

Linda Cardinal, 'Femmes et francophonie: une relecture du rapport ethnicité-féminisme', in *L'ethnicité à l'heure de la mondialisation* (Ottawa: ACFAS-Outaouais, 1992).

Linda Cardinal, 'Théoriser le double spécificité des franco-Ontariennes', in Marie-Luce Garceau, *Relevons le défi* (Ottawa: Les Presses de l'Université d'Ottawa, 1992).

Pat Connelly and Martha MacDonald, 'Women's Work: Domestic and Wage Labour in a Nova Scotia Community', in Roberta Hamilton and Michèle Barrett, *The Politics of Diversity* (Montreal: Book Centre Inc., 1987), pp.53–80.

Vanaja Dhruvarajan, 'Women of Colour in Canada: Diversity of Experiences', in Sandra Kirby et al, *Women Changing Academe* (Winnipeg: Sororal Publishing, 1991), pp.3–12.

Jean Bethke Elshtain, Jean Bethke *Democracy on Trial* (Concord, Ontario: Anansi 1993).

Roberta Hamilton, and Michèle Barrett *The Politics of Diversity: Feminism, Marxism and Nationalism* (Montreal: Book Centre Inc. 1987).

Iacovetta, 'Making New Canadians: Social Workers, Women and the Reshaping of Immigrant Families', in Franca Iacovetta and Mariana Valverde, *Gender Conflicts* (Toronto: University of Toronto Press, 1992), pp.261–303.

Nitya Iyer, 'Disappearing Women: Racial Minority Women in Human Rights Cases', *Canadian Journal of Women and the Law*, 1993, Vol.6, No.1, pp.25–51.

P.Jackson, 'Guest editorial', *Environment and Planning D : Society and Space*, 1991, Vol.9, pp.131–134.

Jane Jenson, 'Gender and Reproduction, or Babies and the States', *Studies in Political Economy*, 1986, Vol.20, pp.9–46.

Danielle Juteau and Barbara Roberts 'Ethnicity and Femininity: d'après nos expériences', *Canadian Ethnic Studies*, 1981, Vol.8, No.1, pp.1–23.

Danielle Juteau, and Barbara Roberts 'Special Issue: Ethnicity and Femininity', *Canadian Ethnic Studies*, 1981, Vol.8, No.1.

Heather Jon Maroney, and Meg Luxton, *Feminism and Political Economy* (Toronto: Methuen, 1987).

Jeannie Martin, 'Multiculturalism and Feminism', in Gill Bottomley et al., *Intersexions: gender, class, culture, ethnicity* (North Sydney: Allen and Unwin, 1991), pp.110–131.

Sheva Medjuck, 'Ethnicity and Feminism: Two Solitudes?', *Atlantis*, 1990, Vol.15, No.2, pp.1–10.

Chantal Mouffe, 'Citizenship and Political Identity', *October*, 1992, Vol.61, pp.28–32.

Roxana Ng, 'Constructing Ethnic Phenomenon', *Canadian Ethnic Studies*, 1981, Vol.8, No.1, pp.97–108.

Roxana Ng, *The Politics of Community Services* (Toronto: Garamond Press, 1988).

Joy Parr, *The Gender of Breadwinners* (Toronto: University of Toronto Press, 1990).

Anne Phillips, *Engendering Democracy* (University Park, Pennsylvania: The Pennsylvania State University Press, 1991).

Geraldine Pratt and Susan Hanson 'Geography and the Construction of Difference', *Gender, Place and Culture*, 1994, Vol.1, No.1, pp.5–29.

Resources for Feminist Research, 'The Lesbian Issue', 1983, Vol.7, No.1.

Resources for Feminist Research, 'Women and Disability', 1985, Vol.14, No.1.

Daiva K. Stasiulis, 'Theorizing Connections: Gender, Race Ethnicity and Class', in Peter S. Li, *Race and Ethnic Relations in Canada* (Toronto: Oxford University Press, 1990).

Stewart, Honston, Beth Percival and Elizabeth R. Epperly, *The More We Get Together* (Charlottetown: Gynergy Books, 1992).

Sharon D. Stone, 'Lesbians against the Right in Toronto', in Jeri Dawn Wine and Janice L. Ristock, *Women and Social Change* (Toronto: Lorimer, 1991), pp.236–253.

Mariana Valverde, 'When the Mother of the Race is free': Race, Reproduction, and Sexuality in First-Wave Feminism', in Franca Iacovetta and Mariana Valverde, *Gender Conflicts* (Toronto: University of Toronto Press, 1992), pp.3–26.

Iris Marion Young, 'Impartiality and the Civic Public', in Seyla Benhabib and Drucilla Cornell, *Feminism as Critique* (London: Polity Press, 1987, pp.56–76.

Iris Marion Young, 'Polity and Group Difference: A Critique of the Ideal of Universal Citizenship', *Ethics*, 1989, Vol.99, No.2, pp.250–274.

The Dynamics of Multi-Ethnicity in French-Speaking Quebec: Towards a New Citizenship

LOUIS BALTHAZAR

As a result of their 'quiet revolution', French-speaking Quebeckers have gradually replaced ethnic consciousness by allegiance to a 'national state' on the territory of the province of Quebec. Two important Charters, one on rights and freedoms (1975), the other on the French language (1977), have marked this significant evolution of Quebeckers' collective identity. Due to specific immigration policies, Quebec is becoming a multi-ethnic society of its own, distinct from the rest of Canada.

Quebec society has become more pluralistic and multi-ethnic than it has ever been. Yet Quebec remains quite distinct from other Canadian provinces, more so than these provinces are from one another. For those who identify themselves as Quebeckers, the essential challenge is to maintain both distinctiveness and pluralism, while intensifying their interconnection and dynamism. Multi-ethnicity must be understood as a result of the profound socio-political transformation that has affected Quebec in the last thirty years. Contemporary Quebec offers a new and dynamic cultural amalgam. One could even go as far as detecting the rise of an original Quebec citizenship that is not perceived as incompatible with Canadian allegiance. Such are the three points to be dealt with in this paper.

Recent Evolution
In the course of their 'quiet revolution', French Canadians living in Quebec (where they constitute the vast majority of the population: over 80 per cent) have somewhat modified their sense of belonging. More or less explicitly, they became more territorially oriented, more conscious of the relevance of provincial territory as a modern communication network. It was realized that Quebec is the only area where such a network could be consolidated and thus allow for the development of a modern French-speaking community. This territorial network would gradually become more important than the bonds of ethnicity that had so far insured survival of the French-Canadian people.

Quebec's Francophones, as a consequence, thought of themselves less and less as a French-Canadian minority and more and more as a Quebec majority. As long as they had perceived themselves as an ethnic minority, they had not expressed any willingness to integrate other ethnic groups, except for a few Roman Catholic Irish or Italian people, mostly as a result of intermarriage. By and large, the so-called 'revenge of the cradles', that is a very high birth rate, was sufficient to conjure up a policy of assimilation that had been cooked up by Lord Durham, a British commissioner, in the mid-nineteenth century. In the 1960s, however, with the full access to modernity, great progress towards secularization and spectacular lowering of the birth rate, the new majority consciousness was soon coupled with a desire to integrate other Quebeckers into the Francophone network. In the Montreal area, particularly, where almost half of the Quebec population is living, the French-speaking majority appeared threatened by growing flows of immigrants who naturally integrated, in very high proportion, to the Anglophone community. The low birth rate had to be compensated with the integration of immigrants.

Quebec was the theatre of what Anthony D. Smith has described as the transition from an ethnic conception to that of a national state, as a result of bureaucratic, economic and educational transformations produced by an emerging state.[1] Between French-Canadian and Quebec identity lies the whole difference between ethnic allegiance and the social contract. By becoming Quebeckers first, Quebec Francophones had to turn automatically towards all the others living with them within the provincial territory: Anglophones and foreign stock citizens. They would move from a traditional conception of the nation based on blood to a modern one based on free will.

Resistance

The transition, however, could not be that fast and simple. First, because Anglophones, including those who had just integrated, were not the least attracted to a Quebec identity. They remained, first and foremost, Canadians, very well conscious of belonging to the country's majority, not at all to a minority in Quebec. Being Quebeckers, for them, did not mean anything but residence and formal acceptance of a particular legal sub-system. They would not take a place within the French-speaking network. Even some ethnic groups living closer to Francophones, like the Italian community in the Montreal North End, offered resistance and called for English schools.

Francophones, on the other hand, tended to remain French Canadians at heart, even when they gradually identified as Quebeckers. Populations do not easily give up their ethnic allegiance. It was therefore a slow process, taking place over a generation, that enabled French-speaking Quebeckers to consider Anglophones and foreign-born people as part of the same society. Thus two antagonistic attitudes confronted each other. The French-speaking majority was demanding the integration of immigrants, as if it could take place unilaterally without any real opening and adjustment on the part of the majority. Minorities remained adamant and even hostile towards the new reinforced Quebec nationalism. Fortunately, with time, attitudes evolved on both sides. The logic of a modern and secular Quebec, which would be at once francophone and pluralistic, gradually forced itself upon people, especially among the younger generation.

Two Universal Charters

The Quebec government has contributed to this new vision in two ways. Two great charters have legally sanctioned the new Quebec's fundamental features: the Charter of Human Rights and Freedoms and the Charter of the French Language.

The Charter of Human Rights was adopted in 1975. It guarantees fundamental human rights in all matters falling under Quebec's legislative jurisdiction. Among other dispositions, it includes a declaration pertaining to the equality of persons and the rejection of all forms of discrimination:

> Every person has a right to full and equal recognition and exercise of his or her human rights and freedoms, without distinction, exclusion or preference based on race, colour, sex, pregnancy, sexual orientation, civil status, age except as provided by law, religion, political convictions, language, ethnic or national origin, social condition, a handicap or the use of any means to palliate a handicap(Art. 10).[2]

There are other provisions in the Charter for the creation of affirmative action programmes to remedy discrimination. A Commission of Human Rights (La Commission des droits de la personne du Québec) is the Charter's trustee. It has the mandate to oversee the implementation of the charter, thanks to large powers of inquiry, mediation and judicial claim.

The French language Charter became law in 1977. It aimed at insuring linguistic security for the French-speaking majority without any prejudice for the linguistic minority. A pluralistic Quebec would keep its cohesion and specificity through its unique North-American Francophone communication network. Bill 101 (the legal incorporation of the Charter) made French the province's official language, without prohibiting the use of any other language. By decreeing that the main idiom of public communication is the French language, the Charter constitutes a unifying device that applies to all Quebec citizens without any discrimination. In this respect, it can be seen in the equalitarian tradition of modern France. One of the primary effects of the linguistic legislation is obviously the integration of immigrants to Quebec's mainstream. Since the law did not apply, for instance in matters of education, to those already settled in Quebec, it could not be said to undermine freedoms. Immigration is a voluntary decision and would-be immigrants are fully informed in advance of the Quebec law.

Immigration Policies

The Quebec government has devoted considerable effort to making sure that such information would be provided for all specific features of the distinct society. Back in 1965, an immigration service was provided within the Ministry of Cultural Affairs. In 1968, the Ministry of Immigration was created. Negotiations were immediately initiated with the federal government so that Quebec could play a role in the selection of immigrants. The objective was to insure better integration for those who would come to live in the province of Quebec.

Several agreements were progressively concluded between both levels of government to allow Quebec to act in a decisive manner (in concordance with Canadian norms) at all stages of the immigration process: selection, reception, and integration. In 1971, Quebec gained the right to be represented abroad by information agents. In 1975, another accord provided for the provincial government to offer non-binding advice to its federal counterpart. The 1978 agreements conferred real power to Quebec at the selection level. Lastly, after the failure in 1990 of the so-called Meech Lake agreements that would have enshrined provincial immigration powers into the Canadian Constitution, an accord was concluded in 1991 between Ottawa and Quebec that gave extensive and exclusive powers to the province. The federal government would keep its prevailing role in admitting migrants and granting citizenship, but Quebec could take over all other responsibilities and receive financial compensation for its role pertaining to reception and integration.

The Quebec Ministry of Cultural Communities and Immigration was merged in 1994 with International Affairs, as a result of an effort to reduce the number of portfolios in the Cabinet. The rationale for the fusion was that the two departments were often related in their functions, especially abroad. However, their objectives have always remained thoroughly different. It is one thing to promote Quebec interests externally, to establish relations with foreign governments or institutions. It is something else to recruit immigrants, to welcome them and to foster the integration of various ethnic groups. The two departments have kept their separate organization, but Immigration has lost some visibility and prestige in the process.

At any rate, this thirty years evolution is quite significant. Starting with a more or less explicit consciousness of a territorial community and a fresh will to strengthen a communication network on the Quebec land, a new conception of openness, inclusiveness and pluralism gradually took shape.

The New Outlook of Contemporary Quebec

It becomes more and more evident in Quebec that new dynamics are at work. But the future of Quebec may appear uncertain. This is still a fragile, insecure society, not very well known by the outside world and subject to the pressures of a uniform conception of Canada that prevails both in Ottawa and in the other Canadian provinces.

There are many Quebeckers who worry about immigration. They resent the high annual level of immigration and are disappointed with the results of the integration process.[3] They are concerned about the future of the French language, particularly in the Montreal area. This kind of apprehension and its by-products, which may be tinged with quasi-racist behaviour, are noticeable mostly among middle-age or older people, who are witness to remnants of the past. Attitudes do not change easily, and unfortunately this sends a message to immigrants in such a way that these fears may become self-fulfilling prophecies: blaming the newcomers for not speaking French may just contribute to their continued reluctance to do so and to join the Francophone community.

Concentrating however on the main trends and observing young peoples' behaviour in particular, one cannot but record an evident movement towards pluri-ethnicity.

Policy Papers

The Quebec government has taken the lead in this respect. In 1990, the department of Cultural Communities and Immigration published a political statement on immigration and integration.[4] The objective was clearly set: to foster substantial immigration that will contribute to Quebec's progress and wealth; to achieve this goal, measures must be taken so that the integration of immigrants will be successful; all Quebeckers must contribute to this achievement.

The policy paper uses the phrase 'Quebeckers from cultural communities' to designate people of diverse ethnic origins (other than French, British or aboriginal) more or less recently settled in Quebec. This could be seen as an enduring manifestation of an old habit to identify people according to their ethnic origin, which is not very conducive to integration. The ministry justifies its wording:

It should be borne in mind that, in a democratic society, the choice of

identifying oneself or not with one's origins belongs to the individual
... Nonetheless, for want of another, more satisfactory expression,
'Quebeckers from cultural communities' will ... be used ... The
notion describes two important sociological realities: on the one hand,
the attachment to their culture of origin experienced by many
individuals and their participation in our society that can be linked, in
whole or in part, with ethnic origin.[5]

This is a realistic assessment, albeit not entirely convincing.

After stating the necessity of immigration to maintain Quebec's
demographic weight and compensate for its low birthrate, the government
paper goes further. Ethnocultural diversity is considered, above all, as a
means of enrichment.[6] It brings forth the notion of 'moral contract' to
describe the integration process. This is not a legal contract but one in which
the host community states a willingness to open up to newcomers, as well
as committing the latter to an acceptance of basic principles underlying their
integration. These principles are related to the social values of a modern
Quebec:

- a society in which French is the common language of public life
- a democratic society where everyone is expected and encouraged both
  to participate and contribute
- A pluralist society that is open to multiple influences within the limits
  imposed by the respect for fundamental democratic values and the need
  for intergroup exchanges.[7]

The paper also recommends an increase in the proportion of French-
speaking immigrants, maximization of the economic impact of the selection
of independent candidates, while favouring family reunification and
maintaining refugee reception.

Strong emphasis is given to the development of an open and welcoming
attitude and the implementation of measures aimed at facilitating the
reception of immigrants. Further recommendations are: better integration to
the labour market, equality of access to housing and adaptation of
institutions to the pluralist reality, as well as fostering the regionalization of
immigration and developing the knowledge and understanding of Quebec
society.

The Council of Cultural Communities and Immigration is an advisory
body created by the government in 1984, composed of independent persons
considered representative of all Quebec's cultural communities. In the
summer of 1993 the council produced an important report on the issue of
'reasonable accomodation' to the needs and wishes of immigrants,[8] with the
objective of removing from the legal process as many minor conflicts as

possible between foreign-born people and some Quebec institutions and organizations. Basic principles were put forward to provide guidelines. Several examples were given to illustrate opportunities for compromise between the imperatives and goals of an organization and the duties, mores or habits of certain cultural groups. 'Reasonable accommodation' was described as an exercise in good relations between two parties in order to 'dedramatize' the perception of diversity.[9] The report stated that, in spite of a few much-publicized confrontations, most problems relating to the integration of immigrants into Quebec organizations and institutions were dealt with through imagination and compromise.

In October 1993, Ms Monique Gagnon-Tremblay, then minister of Cultural Communities and Immigration, published an article in which she stated again the basic values at the heart of the moral contract:

> ...public liberties, the sovereignty of Parliament, the rule of law, state neutrality towards religions, the primacy of the French language, peaceful resolution of conflicts, equality of citizens and henceforth of men and women.[10]

Again in 1993, the Superior Council of Education, another advisory body reporting to the Education minister, published an extensive paper on the reception and integration of pupils (mainly at the primary and secondary level) from the cultural communities. In this paper the Council urged Quebec schools to take responsibility for introducing immigrant children to the fundamental values of Quebec society, enumerating the following elements of the 'common public culture' into which immigrants are to be integrated:

- French as the official language
- A Judeo-Christian cultural tradition, inspired by French, British, American and aboriginal sources
- A legal system based on British common law and French civil law, along with a charter of rights
- A parliamentary democracy based on freedom and equality of citizens
- An economic system that includes private enterprise and state-operated companies.[11]

Multi-ethnicity in Real Life

Beyond governmental and official documents, multi-ethnicity is a fact of life in Quebec. It can be seen daily in the neighbourhoods of Montreal, in labour relations, in schools, in leisure and cultural pursuits. Quebec television witnesses some integration successes. Talk show hosts like Norman Brathwaite (born in Quebec from Jamaican parents), Gregory Charles (born in Quebec of a Haitian father and French-Canadian mother) and Sonia Benezra (born in Egypt) are among the most popular television artists. Although they reflect foreign origins, they are considered by all as authentic Quebeckers. Nathalie Petrowski, Pierre Foglia and Agnes Gruda are columnists in Quebec's largest daily newspaper. This multi-ethnic character is reflected in political life. Osvaldo Nunez (born in Chile) is a member of Parliament in the 'Bloc québécois', the party devoted to Quebec sovereignty. The governing Liberal party of Canada counts several elected members from Quebec who were not born in Canada. At the provincial level, Christos Sirros (Greek origin) and John Ciaccia (Italian) were ministers in the Quebec government up to September 1994. Even the secessionist Parti québécois (forming the government since the fall of 1994) includes many members who are foreign-born. So far, however, it has not had much electoral success in multi-ethnic constituencies, and as a consequence the Quebec government, as of early 1995, is composed entirely of people from French Canadian origins, although at Montreal city hall, the Chairperson of the Executive Council is Ms Noushig Eloyan, a woman from Armenian origin, and the President of the Public Security Commission is another woman, Ms Kettly Beauregard, born in Haïti.

In education, largely as a result of Bill 101 that requires children of immigrants to attend primary and secondary school in the French sector, a great proportion of students in French language schools were born abroad. In the Montreal area, one student out of three registered in Francophone schools has a mother tongue that is other than French. Some 25 out of about 300 Francophone schools report more than half of their clientele as allophones (of a mother tongue other than French).[12] Intercultural education is an object of constant concern in school commissions. There are special sessions to train teachers for multi-ethnic classrooms. Research centres on multi-ethnicity have been created in some universities.

Many social organizations, such as religious groups, trade unions, and popular action bodies, have organized meetings, fora or standing commissions to encourage intercultural fraternity and integration. Diverse ethnic groups are also present in the business community. For example, in 1991 the Vice-President of International Service for the Desjardins Credit Union System (Caisses populaires), Mr Nguyen Huu Trung, declared:

> We are fortunate enough to count on a multi-ethnic labour force that is extremely diversified. This is an asset that our enterprises have not yet fully exploited.[13]

A well known Canadian novelist, Neil Bissoondath – born in India, brought up in Trinidad and a resident of Toronto for many years – provided an interesting testimony in favour of the new multi-ethnic Quebec identity. In a book that provoked strong reactions in English-speaking Canada, he criticized the Canadian policy of multiculturalism for being too centered on the preservation of ethnic identity, and not enough on integration. In Quebec, however, where he settled in the early 1990s, he discovered another approach. He writes:

> ... while English Canada saw its defining Britishness dismantled, Quebec saw its defining Frenchness strengthened.
> For a newcomer, the difference was striking.
> In English Canada, the prevailing attitude seemed to be 'Come as you are – Do as you please'. The society had few expectations beyond adherence to the basic rule of law.
>
> Quebec, however, was more demanding. The prevailing attitude was 'Come as you are, but be prepared to engage with a French-speaking society.'[14]

In spite of this positive note, Bissoondath's enthusiasm remains limited: 'Quebec is no haven for immigrants. It too has its share of racists, and an undeniable strain of xenophobia runs through its nationalism.'[15] He definitely rejects the sovereignty project, even though he recognizes that it may be carried in a pluralistic way. By and large, however, he is optimistic about the dynamics of multi-ethnicity:

> There is a tension in Quebec between the old, racially minded nationalists and their modern, more cosmopolitan brethren. There are many questions, no easy answers – but the debate has been engaged, the hard questions are being asked, and there is a sense that the new is gaining ground on the old.[16]

A public opinion poll, conducted in 1993 by an independent firm for the Ministry of Cultural Communities and Immigration, confirmed that Quebeckers are really on a path towards a 'cosmopolitan' nationalism. It revealed that only 26 per cent of the total Quebec population had no intercultural contact either in their neighbourhood, at work, among their friends or among family members. 46 per cent had friends belonging to a so-called 'cultural community'. 62 per cent believed that immigration could favour economic development. The same proportion thought 'visible minorities' were well disposed towards integration.[17]

It has been frequently noted that a multi-ethnic identity for Quebeckers is mainly a Montreal phenomenon and that positive attitudes towards immigrants are not common in more ethnically homogeneous parts of the province. Of course, it is undeniable that 88 per cent of immigrants settle in the Montreal area. The Ministry's efforts to disperse newcomers throughout the province have so far not been very successful. Nonetheless there has been notable progress in some cities, notably Quebec, Sherbrooke, Hull, and Trois-Rivières. In Quebec city's metropolitan area, for instance, there are 15,000 people not born in Canada. This is not much for a population of 500,000. But it is enough to demonstrate that integration to Francophone Quebec can be quite successful. In 1994, 450 persons, from 65 different countries, received their Canadian citizenship in Quebec city.[18]

It must be kept in mind also that a multi-ethnic picture of society is projected throughout the territory by Quebec television (originating mostly from Montreal). There are also regional university campuses where faculties reflect some ethnic variety, which may be felt by the population. It is therefore the whole of Quebec that is moving towards multi-ethnicity. This move is obviously much slower outside Montreal but there are no signs of resistance from these regions.

A New Citizenship

As a consequence, a new citizenship is emerging. Let us use this term with caution. It must be clearly understood that Quebeckers are Canadian citizens (for the time being) and that, in a strict legal sense, the word 'citizenship' does not apply to the Quebec identity, however distinct and specific it may be. Nonetheless, by taking into account the realities mentioned and analyzed above, there seems to be a typically Quebec way of carrying Canadian citizenship.Some authors have begun to refer to a 'quasi-citizenship'.

> Permanent mobilization of the electorate around themes of national specificity coupled with the progressive extension of internal and external sovereignty is producing a Quebec quasi-citizenship that is superimposed on formal Canadian citizenship.[19]

A Common Public Culture

The notion of a 'common public culture' seems to correspond to this quasi-citizenship. It is used more and more in Quebec to define a new pluralistic identity. It is not the ancestral culture of Quebeckers but a dynamic way of life to be shared by all people living in Quebec. This notion of culture has been characterized by Dominique Schnapper as a process:

> The result of continual negotiations with the external world, through which an identity is affirmed like a horizon, something that can't be defined but by continual creation, the result of individuals' actions and interactions with the global society.[20]

In Quebec particularly, as a result of this recent evolution, identity must be defined as a creation that is more novel than continual. Citizenship must adjust to a more and more heterogeneous population. At the same time, inasmuch as heterogeneity is growing, the necessity of an instrument for society's cohesion and unification is more urgent than ever. Religion, folklore and traditions cannot play this role any more. Language, on the other hand – especially a universal one like the French language – can fulfil this function, as indicated above. French may thus remain Quebec's public language and, consequently, the language of integration. The American example is enlightening in this respect: '... a common language,' writes American historian Arthur Schlesinger Jr, 'is a necessary bond of national cohesion in so heterogeneous a nation as America.'[21] This does not make Schlesinger a supporter of the official unilinguism that was adopted by some states. He does not stand against the use of diverse languages in the United States. But, according to him, a common language is indispensable for the cohesion of a pluralist society. This principle is all the more valid for Quebec where French does not have the assimilation power that English has in the United States.

The culture that will be transmitted through the use of the French language will constitute however a different amalgam from traditional French Canadian culture. It should reflect the contribution of other Quebec communities: anglophone and all the others that gradually modify Quebec's outlook.

Aboriginal (or native) populations are a special case. They claim the right to self-determination. This was recognized, although in a very general way, by the Quebec National Assembly in 1985. They cannot be required therefore to integrate into Quebec's common public culture. That being said, a new partnership may have to be defined between Quebeckers and the eleven native nations living in the province.

Quebec's dynamic and pluralistic culture is shaped by certain values. To those enumerated above that revolve around democracy, the Charter of Rights, and the use of the French language, perhaps can be added a certain sense of community linked to the relatively small size of the Quebec society. This may be reflected by the frequent ties between private enterprise and the government and by the way the economic network operates, notwithstanding its openness to the North American continent and the world at large. In addition the heritage of Christianity may still be marking the culture, in spite of secularization.

As dynamic and future-oriented as this culture may be, it is still rooted in history. Quebec history is certainly susceptible to being revised and revisited. Once forgotten elements, such as the various contributions of different groups, have to be emphasized to promote the objectives of contemporary pluralism so that history may be an essential part of the school curriculum for students of various origins; immigrants, as well as old stock citizens, ought to be sensitized to the history of the society in which they live.

Integration Models

Canadian multiculturalism may have diverted newcomers' attention from the core of Canadian life and its proper history, as Bissoondath has complained. Quebeckers have other reasons to suspect multiculturalism, for it has been presented as if the Francophones' culture was just one of the various cultures that form the Canadian mosaic. No one has dared propose two multiculturalisms in Canada.

This may be why Quebeckers have been more inspired by the French and the American integration models. In both cases, the inspiration is a liberal and voluntaristic conception of the nation according to which anyone is free to integrate but at the same time pressured to adjust to public norms. The French jacobin style of centralization and uniformity has often suppressed differences in a radical and unfair manner. But it has produced a citizenship based on equality and deprived of any reference to ethnicity. Americans have not dealt very well, to say the least, with minorities, such as native Americans, Black people and the Hispanic neighbours. Nonetheless, the melting-pot synthesis, always inspired by an anglo-saxon elite, has been successful enough to attract immigrants from all over the world to a society perceived as the promised land of liberty.

In both countries, however, the integration process is an object of painful revision. In France, some wish to limit if not to stop immigration because of the rising tensions between peoples of European stock and others recently arrived, especially those from North Africa. In the United States, ethnic revival and so-called political correctness have invaded places once considered havens of integration, like the universities. For many among ethnic groups, allegiance to ethnicity is offered as an alternative to national loyalty. Does it mean that integration is no longer feasible in a world where nation-states are less and less relevant?

In France, many institutions that were once channels of integration have lost their cohesion and prestige. But, according to Dominique Schnapper, there are other ways for integration to function, through individuals' participation in collective action:

> This participation may be analyzed along two main lines: the one that runs through relations in the job milieu and protection in society, the other that reflects social intercourse and relations in the family and various social groups ...[22]

France has not lost, by far, its integration power. It still constitutes the most solid nation of Europe, in spite of its inner tensions and the process of europeanization.

In the United States, the ethnic differentiation movement seems to have reached a ceiling. Still the majority of Black people, 'hispanics' and immigrants see themselves first as American. Integration is undoubtedly more respectful of ethnicity but it is nonetheless a continuing phenomenon. Perhaps France and the United States are submitted to the vindication of history because of their former excesses. These two models of integration may never be the same. Probably for the best. In both countries these days differences are better recognized and standardization is less rigid.

Quebec may benefit from these experiences. Even if Quebeckers are not in a position to impose integration in the old French and American manner (far from it), it is important for them to register the failure of classical assimilation. Quebeckers are in the process of learning to respect differences and tolerating the slow pace of integration. That being said, the contemporary trend in Quebec is to formally promote the common public culture in its dynamic form, without false modesty and with all due respect for individuals. The principles on which this culture rests are noble enough to gain the assent of the great majority of those to whom they are proposed.

Naturally there are still problems with the way Quebeckers deal with ethnic diversity, but there is perceptible movement in the direction of a much greater multi-ethnic consciousness. This will shape a new citizenship within a unique society in North America.

NOTES

1. Anthony D. Smith, *The Ethnic Origins of Nations*, (Oxford: Blackwell, 1986).
2. Quoted in Guy Lachapelle *et al.*, *The Quebec Democracy: Structures, Processes and Policies* (Toronto: McGraw-Hill Ryerson, 1993), Appendix I, p.410.
3. Around 35 000 immigrants are accepted in Quebec each year. This is relatively high (although much less than Ontario) for a population of 6.9 million, considering the fact that 88 per cent of immigrants settle in the Montreal area.
4. *Let's Build Québec Together: A Policy Statement on Immigration and Integration* (Montreal: Government of Québec, Ministère des Communautés culturelles et de l'Immigration, 1990).
5. Ibid., p.4.
6. Ibid., p.14.
7. Ibid., p.15. Let us note that, while fostering integration to the French-speaking community, the government does not exclude integration to the English-speaking minority and supports the English-speaking institutions in this context.
8 *La gestion des conflits de normes par les organisations dans le contexte pluraliste de la société québécoise* (Management of normative conflicts by organizations in the pluralist context of Quebec society). (Montreal: Government of Quebec, 1993).
9. Ibid., p.67. This is my translation as well as for all subsequent quotations from sources in French.
10. *La Presse*, Montreal, 13 October 1993.
11. Conseil supérieur de l'éducation, *Pour un accueil et une intégration réussis des élèves des communautés culturelles* (Quebec: Direction des communications du Conseil supérieur de

l'éducation, 1993), p.72. Translated and summarized by Neil Bissoondath in *Selling Illusions: The Cult of Multiculturalism in Canada* (Toronto: Penguin Books, 1994), pp.206–207.

12. Source: Conseil supérieur de l'éducation, 1993.
13. Quoted by Jean-Claude Leclerc in 'Le Québec, société pluraliste', *Revue Notre-Dame*, No. 4, Québec, avril 1993, p.13.
14. Bissoondath, *Selling Illusions*, p.197.
15. Ibid, p.198.
16. Ibid, p.205.
17. *Le Devoir*, Montreal, 1 September 1993, pp.A1-A10.
18. *Le Soleil*, Quebec city, 16 October 1994, p.A-1.
19. Jean Crête et Jacques Zylberberg, 'Une problématique floue: l'autoreprésentation du citoyen au Québec, in Dominique Colas et al., *Citoyenneté et nationalité* (Paris: Presses universitaires de France, 1990), p.424.
20. Dominique Schnapper, *La France de l'intégration*, (Paris: Gallimard, 1990), p.154.
21. Arthur M. Schlesinger Jr, *The Disuniting of America* (New York: Norton, 1993), p.109.
22. Schnapper, p.240.

The Constitution, Citizenship and Ethnicity

PETER H. RUSSELL

Attempts to establish a unitary sense of Canadian citizenship through symbolic engineering at the constitutional level are self-defeating. Canadians must accept that their only basis for a common ethnicity is their continuing engagement in the challenge of maintaining a political community in which they can accomplish significant civic tasks together while respecting their multiple identities.

The Slipperiness of Language

I must begin by acknowledging the slippery nature of the concepts in my title. Even within the western civilization that has used the concepts of 'constitution' and 'citizenship' in organizing its political life, these terms have not had a constant meaning. Not only have the meaning of these terms varied over time from classical Greece and Rome, through the middle ages, to the rise of the nation-state and modern democracy, but even within and among contemporary constitutional democracies, the meanings of these concepts, particularly the ethical expectations attaching to them – what ideally we expect of a constitution and of a citizen – are contested. And this is within the traditions and practices of western civilization where these words have long been important entries in the political lexicon. Which is to suggest that however variable their meaning, the centrality of these terms to political discourse is an ethnic feature of western civilization – if, that is, a civilization can have ethnicity. But can it?

This brings me to the slipperiest term in my triad: ethnicity. What does it mean? When I began to search through the scholarly literature on this subject, I was somewhat comforted to read on the very first line of the first Canadian text I consulted that 'Very few researchers of ethnic relations ever define the meaning of ethnicity.'[1] A political scientist would surely be foolhardy to enter upon terrain where sociologists fear to tread. And this political scientist will not, except to comment on the two kinds of discourse in which the meaning of ethnicity may be at issue.

Social scientists who wish to exchange information about 'ethnicity' need to agree on a common definition if their communications are to have any coherence. But any definition of ethnicity that a particular academy of scholars comes up with to facilitate scientific exchange is unlikely to be satisfactory in the discourse of constitutional politics where, rather than serving the exchange of knowledge, the term is viewed as conferring status. To designate a group as 'ethnic' is to make a symbolic move in the arena of constitutional politics.

Consider, for example, the definition of ethnicity offered by *The International Encyclopedia of the Social Sciences*:

> An ethnic group is a distinct category of the population in a larger society whose culture is usually different from its own.[2]

A social scientist applying that definition to Canada would probably treat all of the following as ethnic groups: Aboriginal peoples, the Quebecois, the English in Quebec and Francophones in the rest of Canada, and immigrant groups that have retained some identity with the countries from which they came. While the immigrant groups, albeit in varying degrees, might accept such a designation, the other groups would surely reject it. Why? Because 'ethnic group' denies the status – the unique constitutional recognition – which these groups as 'nations' and 'linguistic minorities' have striven to maintain in their relationships with a Canadian political community.

The International Encyclopedia's definition of ethnicity, despite the pretention of that volume's title, is essentially designed for American sociology. It fits in with the constitutional history of the United States where, unlike Europe, the nation did not pre-exist the state but instead was defined by the constitution that established the state. This experience yields a paradigm in which the nation itself is not ethnic but is a community within which ethnic groups may be recognized but lack any constitutional status.

Both the American perspective and the European, with its close association of ethnicity with nationality, yield a unitary model of citizenship. According to this model, citizenship connotes membership in a single unified, if not unitary, nation. The Constitution of the nation-state defines the fundamental rights which all citizens share equally and which give them their primary civic identity. In nation-states whose prevailing public ethic is based on this unitary model of citizenship there may be a good deal of diversity, including racial, ethnic, cultural and linguistic diversity, as well as territorial diversity enhanced by a federal scheme of government. But these subdivisions of the national political community either have no constitutional status, or, if they are constitutionally recognized, the citizen's membership in them and allegiance to them are expected to be subordinate to membership in the more inclusive national political community. The sovereign nation state, according to this model, should be based on a sovereign political community of citizens, a sovereign people, united above all by the sharing of a common set of individual rights.

The Charter: An Abortive Attempt to Achieve the Unitary Model

Canadian nationalists, or patriots, who have brooded about the unity of their country, and the meaning of Canadian citizenship, have been haunted by this unitary model. Canadian traditions and experience seem to depart radically – some would say dangerously – from it. It was this unitary model that inspired the Charter of Rights project.[3] Proponents of the Charter were, in effect, attempting to superimpose over the Canadian political community, with all of its deep and historic communal diversity, a layer of common fundamental rights of Canadian citizens. They hoped that participation in these rights would become the Canadian citizen's primary source of identity, and so provide, in the words of the Charter's great helmsman, Pierre Trudeau, 'the common thread that binds us together'.[4]

A look through the Charter and the Constitution Act, 1982 (the larger constitutional instrument of which it was a part) shows how much Trudeau and company, despite their intentions, were forced to concede, grudgingly, to the reality of the Canadian political community's deep diversity. This concession was most explicit with respect to the Aboriginal peoples whose rights Mr. Trudeau just a few years earlier had contemptuously referred to as 'historical might-have-beens'.[5] Section 25 of the Charter states that the rights and freedoms contained in it are not 'to abrogate or derogate from any aboriginal, treaty or other rights or freedoms that pertain to the aboriginal peoples of Canada'. Section 35 of the Constitution Act recognizes and affirms the 'existing' aboriginal and treaty rights of the Indian, Inuit and Métis peoples of Canada. While there was no clear idea in the minds of the non-Aboriginal leaders who agreed to these words as to what they meant, Section 35 at the very least means, as the Royal Commission on Aboriginal Peoples has recently reminded Canadians, that the status of Aboriginal peoples 'as distinct constitutional entities' is reaffirmed in Canada's constitutional arrangements.[6]

The 1982 constitutional changes, as might be expected, given their chief architect's 'magnificent obsession',[7] were much less accommodating of the historic existence of the Quebecois as a distinct national community. Even so, there is one small gesture in this direction in section 59(1) of the Charter. This section made the coming into force of one Charter right depend on authorization by 'the legislative assembly or government of Quebec'. The right in question was that of English-speaking immigrants in Quebec to have their children educated in English. This right, though only one small part of the Charter, nonetheless could have a significant impact on the character of the Quebec people. A measure of the constitution-makers' distaste for this concession was their unwillingness to use the proper name of Quebec's legislative assembly, namely the National Assembly.

Another part of the Charter that appeared to drive a hole in the unitary model of citizenship was its controversial override clause. By permitting provincial legislatures (and the federal Parliament) to set aside fundamental rights for five years at a time, the override acknowledged the federal nature of the Canadian political community. Fundamental constitutional rights to freedom of expression, equality and due process of law need not be the same for all Canadian citizens. Still, it is interesting to observe how carefully the Trudeauites hedged this concession. The override does not apply to the right to vote or to run in federal or provincial elections, to mobility rights or to language of education rights. These are the only rights in the Charter that are to be enjoyed exclusively by Canadian citizens rather than by all who come within Canadian jurisdiction.[8]

The Charter explicitly acknowledges two other ethnic cleavages in the Canadian political community: English/French bilingualism and multiculturalism. Unlike aboriginal peoples and the Quebecois for whom recognition is basically negative and by way of exemption from the Charter, bilingualism and multiculturalism are positively embraced by the Charter. The Charter goes much beyond the 1867 Constitution in establishing English and French as the official languages of governance throughout the federation and for the first time recognizes the educational rights of the official language minorities throughout the country. The Charter's section 27 provides a pathetically vague invocation of 'the multi-cultural heritage of Canadians' as something to be kept in mind in interpreting the Charter.

These elements of the Charter express the constitutional strategy pursued by federal Liberal governments since the 1960s. Sea-to-sea bilingualism was seen as the pan-Canadian nationalist antidote to Quebecois nationalism. Multiculturalism was then adopted as an antidote to official bilingualism, to keep the rapidly growing section of the Canadian population which identifies with neither the British nor French cultures, from feeling, to use Raymond Breton's insightful phrase, symbolically disadvantaged.[9] The rather dismal results of both prongs of the strategy should dampen enthusiasm for symbolic engineering as a method of nation-building.

For the 1982 constitution-makers recognition of bilingualism and multiculturalism seemed not incompatible with a unitary conception of citizenship.The rights which both might generate could, in principle, be individualized and universal. All citizens could benefit from communicating in French or English and all Canadians, even those of British descent – strange as it may seem to many of them – could contribute to multiculturalism. Constitutional bilingualism and multiculturalism, unlike recognition of Aboriginal first nations and Quebec as a French-Canadian homeland, do not challenge the hegemonic claim of a Canadian state to the primary allegiance of its citizens. Not surprisingly it was elites speaking on behalf of the Quebecois and Aboriginal peoples who did not consent to the 1982 constitutional changes. They spoke for peoples whose sense of identity requires recognition of their own nationhood as primary to that of Canada.

Abortive Efforts to define Canadian Diversity

No Canadian needs to be reminded of the efforts undertaken after 1982 to overcome this withholding of consent and fashion a constitutional accord satisfactory to all parts of the Canadian political community – the four conferences with first ministers and Aboriginal leaders, followed by Meech Lake and the Charlottetown Accord. The memory of these constitutional battlefields is painful to vanquished and vanquishers alike. Though in these engagements Canadians failed to define themselves constitutionally in a mutually satisfactory way, perhaps they can extract from these failures some wisdom about the conditions of enjoying a collective life together – of how with all their social complexity and divisions they might share a common citizenship.

One such lesson that might be taken from these experiences is to recognize the hazardous nature – one might even argue the futility – of those constitutional projects that I have characterized as symbolic engineering. The leading example is the proposal in the Meech Lake round to define Quebec, constitutionally, as a 'distinct society'. This language it was hoped would placate Quebec while not offending the rest of the country. Of course, it did nothing of the kind. The calculated vagueness of this phrase failed to deliver the governmental power sought by Quebec autonomists, while the very suggestion that it might give Quebec more power than other provinces was deeply antagonistic to Canadians who visualize their country as a single society united in a federation of equal provinces. Then in the post-Meech round when Aboriginal leaders claimed the status of 'distinct society' for their communities, they offended Quebeckers who felt a proprietorship for a constitutional bauble which, though discarded, nonetheless had been designed especially for them. For a Canadian to recall all of this is to blush.

In the Charlottetown Accord, this effort in symbolic engineering reached comic heights (or depths) in the drafting of a constitutional 'Canada clause' purporting to define the essential characteristics of the country.[10] Little dollops of constitutional status were to be ladled out in amounts that would symbolically gratify all while offending none. The Aboriginal peoples were near the top of the list (right after parliamentary democracy, federalism and the rule of law) as 'first peoples' but were denied the status of nations or distinct societies. Then came Quebec, a 'distinct society' but not the homeland of a founding people. The Canadian federation, the clause went on, was based on the principle of 'the equality of the provinces' all of which had 'diverse characteristics' although only one was distinct. Governments in Canada were committed to the 'vitality and development of the official language minority communities,' though at the same time 'Canadians are committed to racial and ethnic equality', albeit in a society that includes 'citizens from many lands' who contribute 'to the building of a strong Canada that reflects its cultural and racial diversity.' There would surely not be many Canadians, even among the groups actually mentioned, who would find their civic identity summed up in this melange of convoluted and contradictory phrases. Others whose badges of diversity were omitted – women,the disabled and gays, for instance – felt threatened by their exclusion – not to mention the many Canadians who, aspiring to an undifferentiated, unhyphenated Canadian identity, must have been deeply antagonized by this celebration of difference.

Learning to Live With a Fragmented Citizenship
Canadians should learn from this experience just how counter-productive it can be to try to define their collective identity in mutually satisfactory constitutional language. The reality of Canadian citizenship is that at the psychic level it is extraordinarily heterogeneous.[11] Aboriginal Canadians, Quebecois Canadians, Canadians who identify with minority language communities or with ethnic or racial minorities as well as Canadians who yearn to identify with a unified Canadian nation have experienced their connection with Canada historically in very different ways. The value and meaning attached to Canadian citizenship varies across these groups in a quite asymmetrical manner. The constitutional practices and traditions of Canada have no doubt contributed to this psychic heterogeneity. Be that as it may, at this stage in Canada's history, the handiwork of the slickest constitutional wordsmiths can neither overcome nor capture this diversity of civic identities. Indeed, recent experience would suggest that these efforts, however well-meaning, only exacerbate the differences. It is not a matter of trying to put a round peg in a square hole but of trying to put a lot of irregular shaped pegs in one irregular shaped hole.

However unsettling and dissatisfying this asymmetric, discordant, or, to use Alan Cairns' phrase, 'fragmented' sense of citizenship may be to some, Canadians had better come to terms with it because the political conditions that have produced it are unlikely to change in the foreseeable future.[12] If the constitutional status quo does not hold in Canada, the changes that occur are not likely to be in a direction that enhances a unitary conception of citizenship.The most active engines of constitutional change are currently driven by Quebec *independentistes* and leaders of Aboriginal peoples. If either or both succeed in obtaining firmer constitutional recognition of their respective nations, I doubt that this will yield either for them or for the rest of Canada a new basis for a unitary citizenship in autonomous and separate nation-states.[13]

For Aboriginal nations, the social and economic programs their peoples enjoy through their Canadian citizenship will most likely remain ties that bind them to a Canadian political community. Besides, those who have represented the Aboriginal perspective in Canadian affairs have most often emphasized sharing and partnership with newcomers to their lands rather than total political separation.[14] The would-be leaders of a 'sovereign' Quebec indicate their interest in maintaining a close economic association with Canada and perhaps even the continuation of a shared citizenship.[15] If these links were negotiated, their management would require political institutions more integrative than relations between foreign states. However weak or strong such links might be, a 'sovereign' Quebec itself, if achieved peacefully and with the widest consent of all its people, is most likely to be a multicultural and multinational society respecting the Aboriginal nations in its territory and the historic rights of its Anglophone community.

Quebec's moves in an autonomist direction may very well provoke a sharp counter-nationalist reaction in the Rest of Canada. The heat of what Cairns calls ROC nationalism might even rise to the point of terminating official bilingualism and its balancing offset, official multiculturalism. However I doubt that it would become so intense, so tribal, as to force an undifferentiated Canadian citizenship on Aboriginal peoples or so imprudent as to sever mutually advantageous economic ties with Quebec. In addition to the countervailing weight of the Canadian tradition of ethnic and national accommodation, the spectacle of Yugoslavia's tragic unfolding should alert Canadians to the danger of endeavouring to unravel ethnically complex federations into ethnically homogeneous nation-states.

Though a fragmented, asymmetric sense of citizenship is the only kind of citizenship Canadians are likely to share in the future, there are limits to how far it is possible to depart from the homogeneous, unitary model. It is important to address Alan Cairns' challenge to consider how far the constitutional articulation of communal differences can be taken without, in his words, 'destroying our interconnectedness' and our capacity for 'undertaking future civic tasks together'.[16] In other words, how divided and variegated can Canadians become in their civic identities and still share membership in something worthy of being called a political community?

The European Union's Experience

In considering this question, the experience of the European Community or the European Union (as it has been hopefully renamed) can be instructive in its successes as well as its failures.

Let us begin with its successes, which are considerable despite a highly fragmented and thinly developed sense of European citizenship amongst the people of the EU. Most citizens of the European Union identify primarily with their nation-state or some sub-unit of it, such as Catalonia or Scotland. Indeed, European Union citizenship is extended only to those who are, or have become nationals of a member state of the Union. Nonetheless these European Union citizens, through their participation in a larger supranational political community, enjoy benefits which in some respects are still unavailable to citizens of the Canadian federation.

Most of these benefits are consequences of building a single economic market in the European Community. European citizens now enjoy as much if not more economic and social mobility in their union than Canadians enjoy in theirs. Not only have overt and hidden barriers to commerce been removed, but much has been done to harmonize regulatory standards, and, contrary to rumour, not always or even most often, by adopting the weakest regulatory standard.[17] The benefits of progressing towards a single market have by no means been confined to business enterprises and consumers of their products. It is, for example, easier now for university students in the EU to study for a term at a university in another member state and obtain degree credit for the results than it is for Canadian university students to enrich their university education by studying for a term in another province of Canada.

The 'civic tasks' accomplished together by members of the European Union have generally been functional and pragmatic in nature. Most have dealt with aspects of public policy that do not raise social or cultural issues which impinge on national identity. Also, they have been achieved in an opaque, low-key manner through intergovernmental agreements, bureaucratic directives and court decisions. When, in the Maastricht Treaty, European Union citizenship was for the first time and with considerable fanfare explicitly recognized as a formal constitutional principle of the Union, it became considerably more problematic and controversial. This was so despite the fact that the little bundle of mostly political rights tied directly to EU citizenship – participation in municipal and European Parliament elections in any member country, petitioning the European Parliament and ombudsman, and use of member state consular services in foreign countries[18] – had much less practical significance than the wide array of social and economic rights already enjoyed by citizens in the European Community.[19] Nevertheless, when the concept of citizenship in the European Union was raised at the symbolic constitutional level, it became a much greater threat to Europeans whose primary sense of civic identity is with their nation-state. In Denmark in particular, it was a major factor in the public opposition which very nearly led to the rejection of the

Maastricht Treaty in that country.

It has been much easier for the European Union to accomplish civic tasks that are essentially negative in nature such as removing restraints on mobility than to accomplish more positive and creative civic tasks. A common foreign and defence policy, though now a wobbly 'pillar' of the EU, is a far cry from what Canadians, despite the fragmentation of their citizenship, have accomplished in this field. Here, Canadian experience may be instructive to the Europeans in that the support of Canadian citizens for foreign military service has been much more unified since its principal objective has been international peace-keeping. Multi-national states, while less able to raise citizen armies to fight national wars, may have an exceptional capacity to contribute to international peace.

A more telling restriction on the European Union's development relates to community-wide economic welfare – more precisely the reduction of regional disparities. Structural and cohesion funds directed at the poorest regions of Member States were developed by the EC and strengthened in Maastricht.[20] But these transfer payments from richer to poorer regions, as a percentage of public expenditure, are minuscule compared with such transfer payments within the Canadian federation. It is unlikely that there will be much increase in EU cohesion funds until it becomes a more cohesive political community. By the same token, if Canada becomes a less cohesive political community than it has been and the autonomy of some of its constituent parts proceeds further, public support in the better-off sections of the country for a generous level of transfer payments to the poorer regions will likely diminish.

The European Union's largest problem, and some would say its major failure, is, like Canada's, at the level of political institutions. Like Canada, the EU has not found a set of institutions that is sufficiently democratic and efficient for managing the common affairs of such a deeply diverse and fragmented citizenry. The EU has employed a combination of intergovernmentalism and parliamentary democracy, with more of the former than even Canadians have known. This is not the occasion for examining solutions to this institutional problem. However I would hazard a guess that if changes in political institutions are secured for a union that holds in both the EU and Canada, they will take the form of making intergovernmentalism more responsive and accountable rather than the strengthening of a central parliament.

Conclusion

Operating a political community with as fragmented and asymmetric a sense of citizenship as exists in the confederal society of Canada is certainly not easy. As Gibbons and Ponting have observed, had policy analysts with twentieth century social science insights been present at the Confederation debates they 'might well have counselled the abortion of the embryonic concept'.[21] Maintaining a political community, worthy of that name, for a citizenry with multiple identities may not be the easy way, but increasingly it is the way of the world, and it is certainly the only Canadian way.

Canadians have not found, and may never find, a constitutional formula that does justice to the varying identities they collectively harbour. But should they give up the effort of trying to achieve this kind of justice, they would abandon their Canadianness. For it is precisely their engagement in this exercise that gives some grounds for suggesting that Canada's constitutional experience, if not its written Constitution, provides the basis for a Canadian ethnicity – whatever that slippery word means!

NOTES

1. W. Wsevolod, 'Definitions of Ethnicity,' in J.E. Goldstein and R.M. Bienvenue, eds.), *Ethnicity and Ethnic Relations in Canada* (Toronto: Butterworths, 1980), pp.1–15.
2. D.L. Sills (ed.), *International Encyclopedia of the Social Sciences* (New York: Collier and Macmillan, 1965), Vol 5, p.167.
3. Peter H. Russell, 'The Political Purposes of the Canadian Charter of Rights and Freedoms,' *Canadian Bar Review*, Vol.61,No.1 (1983), pp.30–54.
4. *House of Commons Debates*, March 23, 1981, p.8519.
5. Sally Weaver, *Making Canadian Indian Policy* (Toronto: University of Toronto Press, 1981), p.164.
6. Royal Commission on Aboriginal Peoples, *Partners in Confederation* (Ottawa: Canada Communication Group, 1993), p.29.
7. Stephen Clarkson and Christina McCall, *Trudeau and Our Times: Volume I, The Magnificent Obsession* (Toronto: McClelland & Stewart, 1991.
8. The mobility right extends to permanent residents.
9. Raymond Breton, 'Multiculturalism and Canadian Nation-Building,' in Alan C. Cairns and Cynthia Williams (eds.), *The Politics of Gender, Ethnicity and Language in Canada* (Toronto: University of Toronto Press, 1986), pp.27–66.
10. Kenneth McRoberts and Patrick J. Monahan, *The Charlottetown Accord, the Referendum and the Future of Canada* (Toronto: University of Toronto Press, 1993), pp.315–16.
11. For an analysis of how this psychological dimension of citizenship interacts with the legal and representational dimensions of citizenship see Joseph Carens, 'Citizenship and Aboriginal Self-government,' paper prepared for Royal Commission on Aboriginal Peoples, Ottawa, 1994.
12. Alan C. Cairns, 'The Fragmentation of Canadian Citizenship', in William Kaplan (ed.), *Belonging: The Meaning and Future of Canadian Citizenship* (Montreal and Kingston: McGill-Queens University Press, 1993), pp.181–220.
13. In this respect I do not subscribe to Charles Taylor's belief that in Canada the 'extreme positions (of nationalists and antinationalists) always seem to win out here', Charles Taylor, *Reconciling Solitudes: Essays on Canadian Federalism and Nationalism* (Montreal and Kingston: McGill-Queen's University Press, 1993), p.55.
14. James Tully, 'Multirow Federalism and the Charter', in Philip Bryden, Steven Davis and John Russell (eds.), *Protecting Rights & Freedoms: Essays on the Charter's Place in*

Canada's Political, Legal and Intellectual Life (Toronto: University of Toronto Press, 1994), pp.178–204.

15. Daniel Turp, 'Citoyenneté québecoise, citoyenneté canadienne et citoyenneté commune selon le modèle de l'Union européenne,' in Kaplan, pp.164–177.
16. Cairns, op. cit., p.212.
17. Renaud Dehousse, '1992 and Beyond: The Institutional Dimension of the Internal Union,' in Francis Snyder (ed.), *European Community Law* (Aldershot: Dartmouth Press, 1992), Vol. 1, pp.447–474.
18. Hans Ulrich Jessurun d'Oliveira, 'The Citizenship of the Union,' in Joerg Monar, Werner Ungerer and Wolfgang Wessels (eds.), *The Maastricht Treaty on European Union* (Brussels: European Interuniversity Press, 1993), pp.81–106.
19. Elizabeth Meehan, *Citizenship and the European Union* (London: Sage, 1993).
20. Dick Leonard, *The Economist Guide to the European Community* (London: The Economist, 1992).
21. Roger Gibbons and Rick Ponting, 'An Assessment of the Probable Impact of Aboriginal Self-Government in Canada,' in Cairns and Williams, p.188.

Conclusions

WILLIAM SAFRAN

Definitions of membership in the political community, and conditions for entry into it, have varied from country to country and from age to age. These variations have their roots in the different historical experiences and, more specifically, the different circumstances surrounding the building of the political community. Citizenship, which is the legal expression of membership in that community, has been based on both ascriptive and functional criteria. Since the biblical period and the era of the Greek city state, membership in a 'national' community was (as the expression itself implies) determined largely by ascription – birth, descent, and religion – because community was defined in organic terms, that is, was believed to have evolved from extended families and tribes held together by blood ties and other inherited connections. It did not matter whether the existence of such ties could be firmly established; it often sufficed to have a myth of common ancestry, buttressed by a common collective memory and a common cultural or 'folk' patrimony. In some cases, individuals who did not share these commonalities were permanently excluded from full membership in the community; in other cases, it was possible for outsiders to join the community as their progeny adopted the host society's language, religion, myths, and way of life, and married into its families.

The organic, or 'primordialist,' conception of national identity changed gradually as communities grew in size and became more politicized, that is, were redefined in functional, voluntarist, or mechanistic terms. In the case of the large imperial states, the functional aspect was predominant: it was reflected in the obedience of a loyal subject to the commands of an absolute dynastic ruler. To this, Herder and other 'culturalists' juxtaposed the idea of 'natural' national communities, whose collective identities are based on a common cultural-linguistic heritage.

The ideologues of the French Revolution introduced a novel element: an essentially political-ideological approach to the national community. From Abbé Siéyès to Ernest Renan, there was a Jacobin definitional continuity: The nation consisted of all the inhabitants of a territory who obeyed the laws, paid taxes, and performed various other duties required of all citizens. Citizenship was equated with a sharing of sovereignty, which was in turn equated with full participation in a social contract – a *'plébiscite de tous les jours,'* as Ernest Renan put it – and in a common concern with the public interest.[1] In short, the nation was defined in purely political terms, so that *Etat* and *nation* became fused.

Not all nations have accepted the French approach. The Germans have traditionally defined citizenship (*Staatsangehörigkeit*) in terms of *jus sanguinis*, that is, a *Volkszugehörigkeit* based on descent from German ancestors, and they have continued to perpetuate such a definition despite its racist overtones and despite the Nazi policies with which it came to be associated. The British have based entitlement to citizenship on a combination of *jus soli* (birth in the United Kingdom), naturalization, and membership in a society which (like that of the Irish Republic) was once part of the United Kingdom.

The United States, too, has a differentiated approach to citizenship; it combines hereditary and 'deterministic' (*jus soli*) criteria and, with fairly liberal naturalization policies, 'voluntarist' criteria. It should be noted, however, that in fact all these countries have multiple-track and differentiated notions of citizenship which coexist, and the 'organic' element is present in one way or another in all of them.[2]

All these criteria apply to Canada as well, except that the Canadian situation is made complicated by a relatively more differentiated cross-cutting of society. There are the distinctions between the 'Anglos' and the French-speaking Québecois; the native born and the immigrants; and the native born of European origin and the 'indigenous.' In addition, there are rival provincial orientations.

Such divisions have led to varied visions of what Canada is and what it should be. These visions are influenced by the economic and cultural pressures of the large and powerful United States; the occasional cultural interventions of France with respect to Quebec; the changing (and increasingly non-European) origins of the post-war immigrants; and the growing assertiveness of the country's indigenous minorities.

The Canadian case reconfirms the experience of other settler societies where shared socioeconomic activities have helped to shape a civic national consciousness that transcends 'ethnic' consciousness. One of the manifestations of such a civic consciousness is the development of a trans-ethnic sense of fraternity. However, as Laczko's findings demonstrate, feelings of fraternity are selective: they are modified by race and colour and impeded by heterophobic attitudes. Here Canada does not seem to be much different from France, where for many years shared experiences have not been reflected in much fraternal solidarity across the divides of class, religion and ideology: between workers and bourgeois, Christians and Jews, and right and left.

Selectivity has been manifested in particular by Canadian attitudes towards immigrants. Just as the British have spoken of 'belongers', the French of *'immigrés plus facilement francisables'*, the Germans of categories of people who are *'eindeutschungsfähig'*, and US authorities of newcomers who were more naturally 'Americanizable,' many Canadians have maintained a pecking order according to which some immigrants are more apt to become 'proper' Canadians than others. Such selectivity was reflected in immigration policies and exclusions. As Brown has shown in his chapter, the immigration policy of the US, with its Chinese exclusions and its 'national origins' quota system, was paralleled by the Canadian policy of excluding Chinese and, later, Japanese immigrants and (by means of voting restrictions) of maintaining what was in effect a system of first- and second-class citizenships.

Nevertheless, Canada has been more generous and more flexible vis-à-vis its immigrants, and vis-à-vis minorities in general, than the United States. Citizenship may be obtained after three years (compared to a minimum of five in the United States), and naturalized immigrants may hold dual nationality (a privilege granted in the United States only to native-born citizens). Canadians have accepted the idea of dual identity more easily than the authorities in the United States have done, and certainly more easily than they do in France. Whereas the United States accepts a disaggregation of 'citizenship' and 'nationality' only on the (often unarticulated) premise that the 'hyphenated' part of a 'hyphenated' American has little if any cultural meaning, and the French would reject dual national identity altogether,[1] the Canadians openly accept the idea than a Canadian may simultaneously – and normally – be also a Quebecker, a Ukrainian, or a Native Canadian Indian.

Official Canadian policy reflects the acceptance of a distinction between legal citizenship, which is extended to all Canadians and has to do with the right to vote and the duty to pay taxes, and 'societal' citizenship,' which is related to origins, particularistic collective memories, and cultural-linguistic loyalties and preferences. Official policy tolerates, and even encourages, 'associate' or complementary identities: geographic-provincial ones by means of federalism, and ethnocultural ones by means of varied 'multicultural' policies. And multiculturalism in Canada seems to be much more closely related to 'culture' in the traditional sense than it is in the United States, where the term has more to do with affirmative action aimed at diversities of colour, gender, and life-style than with the protection of cultural patrimonies.

How do these policies affect Canadian political unity? The studies by Laponce, Laczko and Kalin of Canadian experience suggest that there is a spillover from the legal to the 'societal'; that ethnic national identity is constructed from above as well as from below; that a pattern of day-to-day 'civic' (that is, political and economic) transactions helps to shape a new kind of ethnic consciousness and a new kind of ethnic nationalism; that multiple community identification does not necessarily have the fissiparous effects so often feared by the French; and that, on the contrary, if citizens are not forced to make an 'either-or' choice between the ethnic and the civic sides of their hyphenated identities, their self-identification in terms of civic nationality tends after a while to predominate. But these findings are hedged with nuances, for identity is subjective and is not always clearly related to origin or socioeconomic function. Thus it is shown that Ukrainian immigrants tend to opt for Anglo rather than Francophone identification and that their children, second-generation immigrants, are more strongly self-identified as Canadian rather than as Ukrainian or even Anglo. Moreover, as Laponce points out, 'citizenship strongly binds the newcomers, but binds only weakly many of the descendants of the *conquered* communities.' Much depends on the benefits or costs associated with Canadian citizenship. According to Russell, the aboriginals have developed strong ties to the Canadian political community because of their consciousness of being recipients of social and economic benefits; conversely, many Quebeckers have harbored ambivalent attitudes about Canadian citizenship, owing to the perception that their community is dominated by Anglos and excessively defined in their terms.

What can we learn from the Canadian experience? Should – or can – the Canadian approach serve as a model for other countries? On the one hand, given the nature of Canada as an immigrant society, it had to be open to a pluralistic approach to citizenship; given the presence of two assertive communities clearly distinguished in cultural-linguistic terms, it had to embrace a multicultural or at least a bicultural-bilingual approach; and given its large territory and its relatively sparse population, it could afford to do so much better than European societies which have hosted immigrants but which are today buffeted by uncertainties about the fabric of their societies. In view of the influx of a more heterogeneous immigration that has challenged traditional notions of national identities, and in view of the development of neo-regionalist sentiments and at the same time supranational sovereignty – both of which have put in question old ideas of the 'nation-state' – there has been a growing need to rethink the notion of citizenship and its connection with ethnicity. Thus the Canadian distinction between legal and societal citizenship might be supplemented and qualified by other kinds of 'functional' citizenship that have come to exist in fact but that need to be legitimated and formalized – for example, social citizenship (the right to social-security protection accorded to residents of a given country); municipal citizenship (the right to vote in local elections accorded to residents of a municipality); and professional-occupational citizenship (the right of resident alien workers to belong to unions and vote in elections to 'corporatist' bodies).[4] The extent to which such approaches affect a given country's sense of political community depends on a number of variables, among them the existing cohesiveness of its society and the strength or weakness of its state. The French state has been strong enough, and its culture and values have been attractive enough, to provide an effective political link for its population of diverse origins, whereas the Belgian state has been too weak to accomplish this. The United States, despite its weak 'stateness',' has furnished enough incentives, both policy-related and symbolic, to heterogeneous ethnic elements to create a new 'societal' citizenship. Canada seems to be in an intermediate situation. This is one of the reasons why it is more difficult to discuss than other cases and why the maintenance of a balance between ethnicity and citizenship represents a particular challenge to that country.

NOTES

1   Ernest Renan, 'Qu'est-ce qu'une nation?' *Oeuvres complètes,* Vol.1 (Paris: Calmann-Lévy, 1947), pp.903–904.
2. See Rogers M. Smith, 'The "American Creed" and American Identity: The Limits of Liberal Citizenship in the United States,' *Western Political Quarterly* Vol.41, No.2 (1987), pp.225–251; and William Safran, 'State, Nation, National Identity, and Citizenship: France as a Test Case,' *International Political Science Review* Vol.12, No.3 (July 1991), pp.219–238.
3. One has only to refer to the decision of the French Constitutional Council, which in 1990 invalidated a sentence in a Corsican autonomy bill that referred to 'the Corsican nation, a component of the French nation'. The basis of the invalidation was the principle that the French nation was 'one and indivisible'.
4. See Gilles Verbunt, 'Citoyenneté, nationalité et identité,' in Catherine Wihtold de Wenden (ed.), *La Citoyenneté* (Paris: Edilig-Fondation Diderot, 1988), pp.239–247.
5   J.P.Nettl, 'The State as a Conceptual Variable,' *World Politics* Vol.20, No.4 (July 1968), pp.559–592.

Notes on Contributors

J.A. Laponce is professor of political science at the University of British Columbia. He is director of the Institute of Interethnic Relations based in the department of Political Science at the University of Ottawa, and is a member of the graduate faculty of Aichi Shukutoku University. Those of his works most relevant to the subject of this issue include *The Protection of Minorities, Languages and their Territories,* and the book he edited with J.W. Berry, *Ethnicity and Culture in Canada: the Research Landscape.*

Robert Craig Brown is professor and Chair of the Department of History, University of Toronto and past president of the Academy of Humanities and Social Sciences of the Royal Society of Canada. He is the author of many books and papers on the history of Canada and of Canadian-American relations.

Rudolf Kalin received his PhD from Harvard University and is currently professor and Head of the Department of Psychology at Queen's University at Kingston. He has been working on multicultural issues with a focus on ethnic attitudes and ethnic identity. He has co-authored (with J.W. Berry and D.M. Taylor) *Multiculturalism and Ethnic Attitudes in Canada*, co-edited (with R.C. Gardner) *A Canadian Social Psychology of Ethnic Relations*, and has published numerous articles on ethnic attitudes, ethnic identity, and evaluative reactions to accented speech.

Leslie S. Laczko is associate professor of sociology at the University of Ottawa. He is the author of a number of articles on language and ethnicity in Canada as well as the forthcoming book *Pluralism and Inequality in Quebec* (New York: St. Martin's Press).

Caroline Andrew is professor of political science at the University of Ottawa. Her areas of research interest are urban development and women and politics. She is the past president of the Canadian Research Institute for the Advancement of Women (CRIAW) and a current board member of the Women's Action Centre against Violence (Ottawa-Carleton)

Louis Balthazar is a professor in the Department of Political Science at Laval University (Quebec city). Among his recent publication are *Trente ans de politique extérieure du Québec, 1960–90* (in collaboration, 1993) and *Contemporary Québec and the United States* (with Alfred O. Hero Jr., 1988).

Peter H. Russell is a professor of political science at the University of Toronto. His research interests are in the fields of constitutional and judicial politics. His most recent book is *Constitutional Odyssey: Can Candians Become A Sovereign People?* (University of Toronto Press, 1993).

William Safran is professor of political science and director of the Center for Comparative Politics at the University of Colorado, Boulder, and president of the Research Committee on Politics and Ethnicity, International Political Science Association. He has authored or co-authored five books and written numerous articles and book chapters on comparative, French, and ethnic politics. The fourth edition of his study of *The French Polity* appeared recently.

INDEX

www.ingramcontent.com/pod-product-compliance
Ingram Content Group UK Ltd.
Pitfield, Milton Keynes, MK11 3LW, UK
UKHW041839280225
455677UK00010B/256